Steel, Smoke & Steam

A COUNTRY ROADS PRESS GUIDE BOOK

STEEL SMOKE & STEAM

A GUIDE TO AMERICA'S SCENIC RAILROADS

MARGERY READ

Country Roads Press
CASTINE · MAINE

For my husband Dick, who has been too busy to finish his model train layout for the past twenty-three years.

STEEL, SMOKE & STEAM:
A GUIDE TO AMERICA'S SCENIC RAILROADS

Published by

Country Roads Press

P.O. Box 286, Lower Main Street

Castine, Maine 04421

COVER DESIGN BY LURELLE CHEVERIE AND GARY RIDSDALE

TEXT DESIGN BY LURELLE CHEVERIE.

COMPOSITION BY CAMDEN TYPE 'N GRAPHICS.

FRONT COVER AND TITLE PAGE PHOTOGRAPHS
COURTESY DURANGO & SILVERTON
NARROW-GAUGE RAILROAD, DURANGO, COLORADO.

BACK COVER PHOTOGRAPHS COURTESY OF
TOP: DUNCAN RICHARDS
MIDDLE: BELFAST & MOOSEHEAD LAKE RAILROAD
BOTTOM: BC RAIL, VANCOUVER, BRITISH COLUMBIA

ISBN 0-9630646-3-0

Library of Congress Card No. 91-077860

PRINTED IN THE UNITED STATES OF AMERICA.

10 9 8 7 6 5 4 3 2 1

FOREWORD

For venturesome travelers who long to watch untrodden back-country glide past their windows, who are fascinated by candid glimpses of the past, who are moved in ways hard to express by the haunting screams of a steam engine whistle, this book belongs in your car or on your coffee table—if not right next to your Bible. It is not only a long backward look through the dramatic history of American railroads, told as only a good storyteller can in terms of colorful heroes and villains, but it is a guide to scores of restored railway lines all over North America.

These venerable rail lines run along great rivers, climb steep canyon walls in Colorado, and fight their way up mountains in West Virginia. They cross high-spidery bridges or steam along forgotten branch lines to pretty villages untroubled by the roar of jets and the monster truck traffic of interstate highways. They can take you to historic places, like Gettysburg and Harpers Ferry, and past scenes reminiscent of the Gold Rush. You can take connecting riverboats on the majestic Connecticut River, passing villages that suggest Currier & Ives prints, or go by train to wineries in the Napa Valley or redwood forests along the California coast where little narrow-gauge engines thread their way through the giant trees.

There is really no end to the enchanting trips offered on these pages, each of them a journey back into the world of our grandfathers and great-great-grandfathers, every one of them an adventure in the American past, and not to be forgotten. If for some incomprehensible reason your imagination is not stirred, put this book down at once before you are hooked. It is already too late for me.

OLIVER JENSEN

CONTENTS

THE ROCKIES: Wars 69

THE FAR WEST: Empires 93

TRAINS EAST

TRAINS SOUTH

TRAINS MIDWEST

MOUNTAIN TRAINS

TRAINS WEST

INTRODUCTION

Here it comes—a black iron dragon with fire in its belly. It hisses steam and belches smoke. It rumbles, huffs, and chugs. And it's **big,** weighing in at about 300,000 pounds. To be that heavy you'd think it had a healthy appetite, and it sure does. It eats coal—up to three tons every hour—and slurps down 5,000 gallons of cold spring water at a gulp. Its boiling heart drives superheated steam through veins of steel.

What is this thing? It's a creature out of legend and a maker of myths, though unlike the unicorn not wholly imaginary. While rarely seen nowadays, it still roams the countryside, and when people see it coming, they get out of the way. Up close, it can be intimidating. Even so, people have been known to travel a long way for a look at this big fellow, and no wonder. It's magic. The sight of it can turn an octogenarian into an eight-year-old. Instantly. In a puff of smoke.

What is this thing? To a world of children—they are the ones most enchanted by its magic—it is known as a choo-choo, a puffer-belly, or on occasion, as a steam engine. Sometimes diesel locomotives are also called choo-choos, which shows the term is less a description than an endearment, and young children are not the only ones who use it. Children of all ages (up to eighty or ninety at least) love railroad engines, steam, diesel, or electric. And everybody—*everybody*—loves trains.

This book is a celebration of steam and diesel dragons. It's also a guidebook to America's most interesting passenger railroads, lines that still survive and prosper. Many of these scenic railroads are small, short-run lines with only a few miles of track, but their venerable passenger coaches roll through some of the most spectacular landscapes on the North American continent.

They also roll through history. It is said we live in the age of the automobile and the airbus, in the era of the rocket and the space shuttle. But did those come-latelies make this country what it is today? No indeed. Ask any old-time railroad man and he'll set you straight. It was steel, smoke, and steam that built up America, that filled up the West with settlers, and spangled the Great Plains with towns.

If you're interested in the past or if you love beautiful country, the scenic railroading experience is for you. Read on and you'll find out how railroading got started, how cowcatchers were invented, how train robber Jesse James outsmarted the Pinkertons, and how Irish and Chinese construction crews pushed transcontinental tracks through the snowy Cascades and Rockies.

You'll also find informative "tickets" for forty-six of the best scenic railroads in the U.S. and Canada. Mind you, these tickets won't actually provide passage on the railroads, but they do provide you with all the information you'll need to plan your next railroading adventure.

ALL ABOARD!

BEGINNINGS

The great American railroading tradition began in the East during the early nineteenth century. Starting in Baltimore, Trenton, Charleston, and dozens of other eastern communities, muscular laborers laid down ribbons of iron-rail track. Felling trees to clear rights of way and driving spike after spike, they joined one town to another and linked coastal cities with the country's undeveloped interior.

These often heroic—and sometimes comic—efforts were spurred on by fortune-seeking entrepreneurs dressed in black frock coats and armed with fistfuls of money—not always their own. Building railroads has always been a risky business and many early lines failed. But others took root. From just a few miles of track, they branched out and grew, eventually forming one enormous, interlocking rail system that tied the East to the West and unified the American nation.

Most traces of these historic beginnings have been lost in a century and a half of improvements. However, for those in search of railroading history, there are reminders of its earliest days. The best way to find them is to experience the history firsthand aboard one of America's scenic short-run passenger lines. Perhaps the most historic of these are in the East, where American railroading was born.

A Shaky Start

In 1815 the New Jersey legislature granted Colonel John Stevens of Hoboken, a Revolutionary War veteran, the first railroad charter, for a line between Trenton and New Brunswick. The legislators wanted to humor the old man. The line was never built, however: No one had devised an efficient way to move train cars over the newfangled tracks. One idea was to put sails on the cars and let the wind power them. Another was to hitch up the cars and have them pulled along like canal boats by teams of plodding mules. Not surprisingly, neither of these methods proved commercially practical, and construction of the first true railroads had to wait for the introduction of the steam locomotive.

The earliest American locomotives drew on English designs but were strong on Yankee ingenuity. In 1830 Peter Cooper, a manufacturer and inventor, built the first U.S. steam engine, which he called Tom Thumb because of its diminutive size. "I had an iron foundry, and some manual skill in working in it, but I couldn't find any iron pipes," said Cooper, describing his effort to build the engine. "The fact is, there were none for sale in this country. So I took two muskets and broke off the wood part, and used the barrels for tubing to the boiler." Cooper then set himself up in a coach-maker's shop and completed his little steam engine. Named for a legendary English dwarf, the Tom Thumb rattled, clanked, and wheezed, but soon proved it could pull a load over a track more efficiently than horses, mules, or the wind. Cooper proved the practicality of his engine when it won a race on the rails of the new horse-drawn Baltimore & Ohio Railroad.

With the invention of the so-called "iron horse," investors and speculators all over the East clamored for the right to build railroads. Maryland, Massachusetts, South Carolina, and many other states granted charters to hastily formed railroad companies. Sometimes, though not always, the charters were followed by construction of actual railroads.

Opportunity, that's what railroads represented, a chance for business interests to make big money and for villages to transform themselves into towns and then cities. Investors began to think of the rails as the road to riches. With charters in their hands, businessmen sold thousands of shares of stock, but the money they raised was not always wisely spent. For instance, it took local promoters several decades to fire up the boilers

Amid billowing steam, an engineer on the Arcade & Attica Railroad (Arcade, New York) makes a final check before pulling out. DUNCAN RICHARDS.

of the Arcade & Attica line in New York, as one unscrupulous organizer after another rolled into town and then out again with well-lined pockets. The efforts of the Arcade citizenry itself eventually paid off, however. Their little rail line finally got moving in 1881, and you can still ride it today (see page 19).

At least 200 railroads were planned or underway by 1837. By 1840, some 5,000 miles of track stretched to the north, south, and west. About a thousand of these miles crisscrossed Pennsylvania while another thousand served New York.

Service on these early lines was extremely primitive by today's standards. They were grimy, bumpy, uncomfortable, dangerous, and seldom on schedule, but they worked. Their tiny, wheezing engines hauled short, soot-blackened wooden passenger coaches or boxy freight cars over shaky tracks and—most of the time—reached their destinations.

The blur of wheels and the hiss of steam convey the essence of railroading. BRUCE ROBERTS.

As if to compensate for their shortcomings, the fledgling railroads often selected grandiose names that began with the word "Great" and ended with "& Western" or "& Pacific" regardless of the fact that the ocean lay thousands of trackless miles to the west. The *New Englander Magazine* aptly expressed the spirit of the age: "We must not forget that the Railroad is but one step in the ascending staircase on which the races are mounting, guided and cheered by heavenly voices. . . . We only mark the beginning."

Although the English built the first locomotives and railroads, the grand scale of American geography combined with Yankee inventiveness and business acumen to make this country first among railroading nations. Whistles, cowcatchers, signals, mail trains, cattle cars, oil tankers, punched tickets, and timetables were all introduced by American railroads.

Whistling While They Work

As any child knows, railroad engines have a voice and a language all their own. Two short toots mean the train is now starting. When approaching a crossing, the engineer gives two long calls, a short, and then another long, which draws out the warning. And that far-off, pensive call floating across the countryside on a summer evening? That's just a sigh much like you might hear from grandfather when he sits in his rocking chair on the front porch. To most Americans a distant whistle says "train," and to the romantics among us, it also says "America." Many scenic trains still use the old steam whistles, and hearing them up close is one of many good reasons to ride.

The earliest steam whistles were simple and could only sing one note. They were introduced during the 1830s by a gentleman appropriately named George Washington Whistler on engines manufactured in Lowell, Massachusetts. One Long Islander, hearing the whistle on the Lowell engine Hicksville as it steamed through Jamaica, New York, complained that it made a "shrill, wild, unearthly sound something like drawing a flat saw across a bar of iron."

When the Erie Railroad broke through the Pile Pond region near Callicoon, New York, many residents of this back-country region hadn't heard the railroad was coming. The new line's first locomotive, the Pioneer, created a stir by sounding its whistle. The shrill call echoed through the mountain hollows and brought startled settlers out of their cabins with hunting rifles in hand. The mountain men figured they should hunt down this new varmint before it caused any trouble. John Quick, a famous trapper just across the line in Pike County Pennsylvania, heard the whistle and rushed out to set a string of traps—big ones—to catch the snorting, steaming behemoth. It is unclear what Quick intended to do with the locomotive had he managed to snare it.

The tale is told of two backwoodsmen drawn down from the mountains by the sound of a distant train whistle. The mountain men found the tracks, but were terrified when they saw the engine coming. They ran for their lives. One of them veered into the woods, while the other took off straight down the tracks. The woodsman on the tracks called out to his friend, "If you can't outrun it on this pretty road, how can you beat it runnin' in the woods?"

A Pennsylvanian told of the first train whistle heard in his neck of the woods. When word got around that the county's first train was on the

A steely freight-car "truck" from the Erie Railroad. DUNCAN RICHARDS.

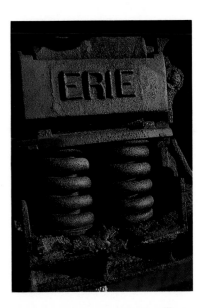

The Gettysburg line runs alongside a quiet road in Pennsylvania.
COURTESY GETTYSBURG RAILROAD.

way, "Everybody came from a distance with all kinds of conveyances. They drove as near as they could get, only looking for the best position to get a view of the train. As it approached [and the whistle blew], the horses took fright and wheeled, upsetting buggies, carriages, and wagons, and it is not now positively known if some of them have yet stopped."

When engineers were permanently assigned to engines, they sometimes modified the equipment to suit their particular needs and personality. Some even had their own distinct whistle calls. John Luther "Casey" Jones had a six-pipe whistle like a calliope on Engine 382, and every field hand from Chicago to New Orleans was familiar with Casey's call. It reached a crescendo and then tapered off to nothing: KA-A-A-SEEEE Jo-o-o-ones.

Catching Cows and Gilding Tigers

Cowcatchers added a distinctly American profile to trains in the U.S., probably because free-ranging stock was not a concern in Europe. In America, however, cows, horses, and buffalo were constantly wandering onto the tracks causing delays and derailments and sparking lawsuits filed by irate farmers whose livestock had been maimed. And animals were not the only ones who got hurt; the open engineer's platforms of early engines were not much protection when a bull charged a train.

Loose livestock was a serious hazard for railroads in both the East and the West. The tracks of the Camden & Amboy line in New Jersey became so crowded that a separate set of wheels was added in front of the engine to support a wicked-looking array of sharp spikes. Unfortunately, this device proved even more successful than its inventors had hoped. On one run, a particularly belligerent bull was impaled on the spikes and had to be removed with a block and tackle before the train could continue. All too literally a "cowcatcher," the spikes skewered

more animals than they swept aside. Learning by trial and error, railroaders eventually modified the cowcatcher into its classic wedge shape. You'll see old-fashioned cowcatchers on the engines of some of today's scenic railroads such as the Arcade & Attica in New York (see page 19) or the Conway Scenic Railroad in New Hampshire (page 18). If local cows linger a bit too long on the tracks, you may even see a catcher in action.

Early engines were more than just functional. Many were gaily

The Blue Mountain & Reading crosses a beautiful stone bridge near its hometown in eastern Pennsylvania. PHOTO BY TOM NEMETH; COURTESY BLUE MOUNTAIN & READING RAILROAD.

decorated, sporting gilt and brass on their wheels, ornamental scrollwork on their cabs, and colorful murals on their boilers or on the sides of cars. For example, the Baldwin Tiger, built for the Pennsylvania Railroad in 1856, flaunted gilt and blue ribbons on its tender, a jungle scene on its headlamp, and of course, a bright orange tiger under the window of the cab. The engine itself was French blue with scarlet and brass trim.

Usually engines boasted names in keeping with their reputations and glorious decorations. Was it fast? Then call it Rocket, Racer, Stampede, or Cyclone. Strong? Then name it Hercules or Sampson. There were Indian names like Uncas and Hiawatha, names taken from mythology such as Jupiter and Adonis, and historial names like Hannibal and Attila. The names of some engines hinted at the financial condition of their owners—Frugality (railroads are an expensive business) or Trustee (a business that led frequently to bankruptcy).

It was Commander Cornelius Vanderbilt, one of history's most successful railroad tycoons, who put an end to all the pomp. As good at pinching pennies as turning up millions, Vanderbilt believed his New York Central employees wasted too much time polishing brass and cleaning the soot from glittering engines. So he decreed that all engines be painted black. He also banished brass—except, of course, from his own private car. Other capitalists soon followed Vanderbilt's example so that more and more locomotives wore only honest, hard-working black.

On the Oil Creek & Titusville in Pennsylvania (see page 23) you can see a working mail car in operation, and at the California State Railroad Museum (page 113), you can even help sort mail. These pleasures remind us of the importance of railroads as mail carriers. Until the advent of the locomotive, the nation had never seen its mail delivered so fast. Nor has it since the government abandoned railway mail cars in this century.

In 1838 President Van Buren signed a bill making every rail line a mail carrier. Mail sacks were hung on high hooks to be snatched on the fly by passing trains. The mail remained locked in pouches to be sorted at the next post office. But Chicago postmaster George Armstong had a better idea. He proposed the mail actually be sorted on the train. To demonstrate the concept, Armstrong had a railroad car modified to serve as a mail car. Accompanied by skeptical newspaper reporters who were sure letters would be blown clear to Kansas, Armstrong carried out the first successful railway mail run in 1864.

Hooking mail sacks on the fly and sorting mail by lamplight all through the night, railway mail clerks were seen as romantic figures. Frequent robberies made the occupation a hazardous one, and since the mail car was positioned far forward on the train, it was likely to be crushed, derailed, or set ablaze in a wreck. Demanding better wages for

A Post Office on Rails

his clerks in 1897, Post Master General Thomas James described the occupation as follows: "The mail clerk must know no night and no day. He must be impervious to heat and cold. Rushing along at the rate of forty or fifty miles an hour, in charge of that which is sacred—the correspondence of the people—catching his meals as he may; at home only semi-occasionally, the wonder is that men competent to discharge the duties of so high a calling can be found."

Near Rochester, New York, the Ontario-Midland steams past a field of autumn pumpkins. DUNCAN RICHARDS.

God's Time or Railroad Time?

Until the railroads gave us standard time, travelers who feared they were running late for an appointment might just as well squint up at the sun as take out a watch. That's because their watches were set according to local times that might vary as much as two hours from one town to the next. Most people measured their days by what some referred to as "God's Time"—whatever the big clock on the local church steeple happened to say. Before the advent of trains, time changes from town to town and city to city were less noticeable, since travel wasn't fast enough to point out the discrepancies. Who cared what time it was in St. Louis if you were headed there in a covered wagon? Powerful steam locomotives and speeding passenger trains changed that attitude.

The earliest published schedules and timetables were often more confusing than helpful—today's travelers might sympathize. Whose time were passengers and engineers supposed to follow? Noon in Washington, D.C., was twelve minutes later than in New York City, and careful travelers riding from Boston to San Francisco might change the hands on their pocket watches twenty times on the trip. Since the various railroad lines kept time according to their own preferences, big train stations could be especially maddening for travelers. The Buffalo depot had three large clocks—one on New York City time to show the comings and goings of the New York Central, one on Columbus, Ohio, time favored by the Michigan Central, and of course, a third showing local Buffalo time. In Pittsburgh a total of six clocks and conflicting timetables kept passengers and dispatchers scratching their heads.

Under pressure from an exasperated traveling public, the railways moved to clear up some—though certainly not all—of the confusion. They took it upon themselves to carve up the country into four distinct zones. According to their plan, depot clocks everywhere within a given zone would always read the same. The concept of time zones had been around for years, but the complications of standardizing time seemed so daunting that the railroads had at first opposed the idea. Their scheduling problems became so horrendous, however, that railroad officials eventually felt they had no choice. Congress seemed unlikely to act on the matter, so at noon on November 18, 1883, the railroads took time into their own hands by establishing the Eastern, Central, Mountain, and Pacific time zones.

As noon approached on the appointed day, the eyes of stationmas-

God's time or railroad time? It was anybody's guess until the railroads established standard time zones from coast to coast. BRUCE ROBERTS.

ters across the country turned to their depot clocks. In Chicago at the West Side Union Depot, which served the Burlington, Pennsylvania, Alton, and Pan Handle railroads, a crowd of engineers, conductors, and signalmen gathered beneath the big wall clock, their timepieces open in their hands. Depot Master Cropsey held a magnifying glass above his big silver watch to better mark the seconds. Precisely at noon, the clock was stopped. At exactly 9 minutes and 32 seconds after the hour—by Chicago reckoning—a telegraphed signal from an observatory in Allegheny, Pennsylvania, told Cropsey to restart the station clock. Now it was noon again at the Union Depot and at train stations throughout the new Central time zone. According to a *Chicago Tribune* reporter on hand to cover the event, "a general murmur of satisfaction ran through the room" as the station clock was now official again and trains could depart "on time."

Newspapers across the country had a field day with the change-over. In New York the *Herald* noted that anyone who "goes to church in New York on November 18 will hug himself with delight to find that

The Ontario-Midland near Fairville Station, New York. DUNCAN RICHARDS.

the noon service has been curtailed to the extent of nearly four minutes, while every old maid in Boston will rejoice to discover that she is younger by almost sixteen minutes."

Even for the railroads, the transition created a whirlwind of confusion, but luckily, no train collisions. Fearing that possibility, the Louisville & Nashville issued a blanket order to all engineers: "Should any train or engine be caught between telegraph stations at 10 AM on Sunday, November 18, they will stop at precisely 10 o'clock wherever they may be and stand still and securely protect their trains . . . until 10:18 AM and then turn their watches back to precisely 10 o'clock, new standard time, and then proceed . . . to the first telegraph station where they will stop and compare watches with the clock and be sure they have the correct new standard time before leaving. . . ."

While schedule-makers smiled (their lives had suddenly become much simpler) many ordinary Americans were hostile to the notion of time zones. What right had the railroads to tell them how to set their clocks? In Bangor, Maine, Mayor Dogberry threatened to have his

Stately Victorian architecture, vintage rolling stock, and spectacular scenery await visitors to the Conway Scenic Railroad in New Hampshire. DUNCAN RICHARDS.

The "age of steam" is reflected in a New York State pond as an Arcade & Attica sightseeing train puffs by. DUNCAN RICHARDS.

constables prevent sextons from ringing church bells or changing steeple clocks in keeping with the new and "unspeakable" time. In Tennessee, a country preacher issued a dark warning to the Louisville & Nashville—don't ignore God's Time. Standing in the pulpit he pounded his watch to pieces with a claw hammer. "Damn old Vanderbilt!" he shouted. "We want God's Time!"

Since they had not initiated it themselves, government bureaucrats were lukewarm to the new timekeeping system. The U.S. attorney general ordered government departments not to adopt the system, but it was soon begrudgingly accepted by federal officials—who were missing too many trains. It was not until World War I that the government legally endorsed the system by passing the Standard Time Act, but by then, the time zones were recognized nearly everywhere in the nation. Evidently, ordinary Americans were far less interested in laws than in railroad schedules. Like their government officials, they hated to miss trains.

How many pocket watches have been set by the whistle of the 10:55 express or the 1:15 mail train? No one will ever know. But decades before the coming of standard time Henry David Thoreau noted that a powerful link between time and trains had developed in the minds of his fellow citizens. "The startings and the arrivals of the cars are now the epochs in the village day," said Thoreau. "They go and come with such regularity and precision . . . that the farmers set their clocks by them, and thus one well-conducted institution regulates a whole country."

Valley Railroad Company

WHERE TO BOARD:
Exit 69 off I-95, then 3 miles North on Route 9 to Exit 3. Two hours from New York City and 2 hours from Boston.

FOR TICKET INFORMATION:
Valley Railroad, P.O. Box 452, Essex, CT 06426. Telephone 203-767-0103 weekdays 9:00 a.m.–5:00 p.m.
North Cove Express: Dinner Train information and departure time, call 203-621-9311.

FARES IN 1992:

	Adults	Children 2–11
Train Only	$7.50	$4
Train & Boat	$11.50	$6
Parlor Car extra fare	$3.25	$3.25

Group rates available for 25 or more.

LENGTH OF TRIP:
Train only—1 hour round trip. Train & Boat—2¹/₂ hour round trip.

DATES OF OPERATION:
May through December.

SCHEDULE:
May 2 through June 10

Sat., Sun., Memorial Day	11:45 a.m. and 1:15, 2:45, & 4:15 p.m.
Wednesdays	2:00 & 3:30 p.m.

June 13 through September 7

Sat., Sun., July 4, & Labor Day	10:30 & 11:45 a.m. and 1:15, 2:45, 4:15 & 5:30 p.m.
Mon.-Fri.	10:30 & 11:45 a.m. and 1:15, 2:45, & 4:15 p.m.

September 9 through November 1

Wed.-Sun.	11:45 a.m. and 1:15, 2:45, & 4:15 p.m.
Columbus Day weekend (October 10, 11, 12)	10:30 & 11:45 a.m. and 1:15, 2:45, & 4:15 p.m.

November 28 through December 20—Christmas train

Sat. & Sun.	1:15, 2:45, 4:15, 5:45 & 7:15 p.m.
Thur. & Fri.	5:45 & 7:15 p.m.

■ The big black engine is all fired up. Passengers hurry out from the old depot to climb aboard and settle themselves on the plush seats. "Boooard!" the conductor yells. The whistle toots twice. Black smoke belches from the smokestack and the brakes let off a hiss of steam that clouds the shrieking wheels.

Up in the engine, the fireman opens the firedoor to shovel on more coal. As the engineer eases open the throttle, the engine begins to chug out of the station, taking on a familiar rhythm. Through meadows, marshes, woodland and farmland, the train picks up speed. Small passengers in the parlor car press their noses to the windows to watch swan families in the spring wetlands or fall color flickering by. The old New Haven tracks hug the Connecticut River's rolling green hills and wide blue waters.

At Deep River Landing, passengers may transfer to a waiting riverboat for an hour's cruise along the river, past turn-of-the-century actor William Gillette's Castle and the Goodspeed Opera House. Picnicking passengers wave at the river traffic and the riverboat exchanges whistle greetings with Selden III, the oldest continuously operating ferry service in the United States.

Back on board the Valley Railroad, children rush to windows on the other side for new sights on the trip home. Diners enjoy lunch or dinner in the elegantly appointed 1920s dining cars. And passengers in the coaches and parlor car watch the green Connecticut hills rush by and the old depot come into sight again.

A final warning blast of the whistle clears the tracks for the start of a journey along the salt tides edging Belfast Harbor and up the banks of the Passagassawaukeag River. The train then plunges into lush green forests and across fields cleared by some of New England's earliest settlers, and on into the town of Brooks.

The B&ML, one of only three municipally owned railroads in the country, offers a lovely way to see Maine, especially in the fall. The railroad staff and crew are particularly friendly and willing to initiate youngsters into the joys and mysteries railroading.

The line's history reaches back to 1867, just after the Civil War. Like many small railroad companies, this one ran out of money before it was completed. In spite of its name, the line never reached Moosehead Lake, but even today the B&ML still has plans for expansion. Presently offering scenic diesel rides in the summer, it hopes eventually to connect with Bangor-to-Boston trains and reinstate regular passenger and freight service.

BELFAST & MOOSEHEAD LAKE RAILROAD

WHERE TO BOARD:
11 Water Street in Belfast. Belfast is one hour south of Bangor on Rte. 1A, and 2½ hours north of Portland via I-95 & Rte. 3.

FOR TICKET INFORMATION:
Belfast & Moosehead Lake Railroad Company, 43 Front Street, Belfast, ME 04915. Telephone 207-338-2330.

FARES IN 1991:
Adults $10.00; Seniors (60+) $9; Children 2–12 $7.50. Children under 2 ride free.

LENGTH OF TRIP:
25-mile, 2½ hour round trip, Belfast to Brooks.

DATES OF OPERATION:
March to October.

SCHEDULE:
Summer Service: 11:00 a.m. & 2:30 p.m.
Write for Spring and Autumn schedules.

Children love the sights and sounds of steam trains. These three are ready for a ride on the Belfast & Moosehead Lake Railroad in Belfast, Maine.
COURTESY BELFAST & MOOSEHEAD LAKE RAILROAD.

CAPE COD SCENIC RAILROAD

WHERE TO BOARD:
Downtown Hyannis Station at Main and Center streets.

FOR TICKET INFORMATION:
Cape Cod Scenic Railroad, 252 Main St., Hyannis, MA 02601.
Telephone 508-771-3788

LENGTH OF TRIP:
1³/₄ hour round trip.

DATES OF OPERATION:
Weekends in May; daily except Mondays from June 1 through October 20.

SCHEDULE:

NORTHBOUND

Train No.	101	103	105	107*
	Continental Breakfast Avail.	Lunch Available	Snacks Available	Dinner Train
LV Hyannis	10:00 a.m.	12:30 p.m.	3:00 p.m.	6:30 p.m.
LV Sandwich	10:37 a.m.	1:07 p.m.	3:37 p.m.	7:07 p.m.
AR Sagamore	10:45 a.m.	1:15 p.m.	3:45 p.m.	7:15 p.m.

SOUTHBOUND

Train No.	102	104	106	108
	Continental Breakfast Avail.	Lunch Available	Snacks Available	Dinner Train
LV Sagamore	11:00 a.m.	1:30 p.m.	4:00 p.m.	7:45 p.m.
LV Sandwich	11:10 a.m.	1:40 p.m.	4:10 p.m.	7:55 p.m.
AR Hyannis	11:45 a.m.	2:15 p.m.	4:45 p.m.	9:30 p.m.

*DINNER TRAINS operate certain evenings. Call for information and reservations.

■ Leave your car behind and see the Cape the way everyone used to— from a train. You can board in Hyannis or Sandwich and ride through the Great Salt Marsh, past cranberry bogs, and beside the Cape Cod Canal. Since the train offers a dining car, you can enjoy a meal while you ride along the graceful curve of Cape Cod Bay. The Cape's sandy spiral was created thousands of years ago by retreating glaciers. As any school child knows, it was a stopping-off point for the Pilgrims on the Mayflower who eventually settled in Plymouth. Especially when combined with a visit to the Glass Museum and Heritage Plantation in Sandwich, the train is a great introduction to the Cape and its fascinating history.

One of the most beautiful Victorian depots in the East awaits passengers of the Conway Scenic Railroad. The skillful carpentry crews of the Portsmouth, Great Falls & Conway built fine depots all along the line, but they saved their best efforts for the summer resort town of North Conway. Designed by a noted architect and completed in 1874, the handsome structure features twin towers overlooking the village park, and separate waiting rooms for ladies and gentlemen. The rail terminal boasts a roundhouse, an operating turntable, a freight house, mail bag stanchions, and a section car house, all on the National Register of Historic Places.

Soon after Alexander Graham Bell and his famous assistant John Watson invented the world's best-known conversation piece—the telephone—they tested it at North Conway. The two men tried to talk to each other over the long-distance telegraph wires strung 143 miles from Boston to the North Conway railroad ticket office. The results proved far less than satisfactory. "We could hear each other over the wire," Watson reported, "but the telegraph line was in such bad shape with its high resistance and rusty joints that the talking was unsatisfactory to both of us." Fortunately, long-distance service to North Conway has improved markedly since 1876.

Today the Conway Scenic operates a seven-mile route between North Conway and Conway over tracks first laid in 1872. The forest and mountain views along this line are spectacular, especially in the fall. The depot in North Conway features a museum and over fifty pieces of rolling stock.

CONWAY SCENIC RAILROAD

WHERE TO BOARD:
Station located on Route 16 at Norcross Circle in the village of North Conway.

FOR TICKET INFORMATION:
P.O. Box 1947, No. Conway, NH 03860.
Telephone: 1-800-232-5251 or (in NH) 603-356-5251.

FARES IN 1992:

	Coach	"Gertrude Emma"
Adults	$7.00	$9.00
Children, 4–12	$4.50	$6.50
Children under 4	Free*	$3.00
Group rates available.		

LENGTH OF TRIP:
11 miles round trip from North Conway to Conway and back.

DATES OF OPERATION:
Opening April 18, 1992. Weekends in April through early June, and early November through late December. Daily from early June to late October.

SCHEDULE:

	Train departs at
April 18–19 & 25–26	11:00 a.m. & 1:30 p.m.
Weekends May through early June	10:00 a.m., Noon, 2:30 & 4:00 p.m.
Daily, early June thru late October	10:00 a.m., Noon 2:00 & 4:00 p.m.
Weekends, early November thru late December	11:00 a.m. & 1:30 p.m.

Sunset Special departs at 6:30 p.m. every Tuesday-Wednesday-Thursday and Saturday during July and August.

SPECIAL EVENTS:
Mother's Day, Father's Day, Birthday, Boston & Maine Railroad Historical Society, Annual Railfan's Day, Turkey Trotter, Santa Claus Express.
*Restrictions apply.

ARCADE & ATTICA RAILROAD

WHERE TO BOARD:
Arcade is three miles east of Route 16, midway between Buffalo and Olean, NY. All trains depart from the orange depot in the center of town where Route 39 joins Route 98.

FOR TICKET INFORMATION:
Arcade and Attica Railroad, 278 Main Street, Arcade, NY 14009. Telephone: (716) 496-9877.

FARES IN 1991:
Adults $8.00; Children (3–11) $4.00
Group rates available. (25 or more)

LENGTH OF TRIP:
15 miles, ninety minutes.

DATES OF OPERATION:
Saturdays, Sundays, & holidays from Memorial Day weekend thru October, plus Wednesdays in July and August.

SCHEDULE:

Decoration Day Weekend	Sat.–Mon.	12:30 & 3:00 p.m.
June	Sat. & Sun.	12:30 & 3:00 p.m.
July & August	Sat.–Sun. & Wed.	12:30 & 3:00 p.m.
Sept. & Oct.	Sat.–Sun., Labor Day & Columbus Day	12:30 & 3:00 p.m.
Fall Foliage	1st, 2nd & 3rd weekends in October	Noon, 2:00 p.m. & 4:00 p.m.

Few railroads anywhere took so long to get rolling as the Arcade & Attica. Financial reversals—some caused by fast-talking scoundrels—and a plethora of other difficulties delayed construction for almost three-quarters of a century. While the A&A's problems were extraordinary, its history of startups, bankruptcies, and takeovers typifies the problems encountered by backers of small railroads.

The line finally got the steam up in its locomotives around the turn of the century. After that it did fairly well until 1951, when it took in only $1.80 in passenger revenue. However, it is doing much better nowadays, and continues regular operation as a successful freight and steam excursion railroad.

The A&A's equipment is especially interesting and historic. It includes a ninety-ton American Locomotive 2-8-0 built in 1920. This big steam engine carries six tons of soft coal and 6,000 gallons of water. There is also a Baldwin 4-6-0. The numbers 2-8-0 and 4-6-0 describe the wheel arrangement on the engines according to a steam locomotive classification system devised by engineer Frederick Whyte. The first digit indicates the number of wheels on the locomotive's leading truck, the second is for the big drive wheels under the boiler, and the third is for the wheels on the trailing axle. Many locomotives, such as the two mentioned above, had no trailing wheel, hence the "0."

The A&A is a National Historic site. When you visit the railroad's Arcade station, be sure to explore President Grover Cleveland's filigreed honeymoon car known as the Warwick.

Picking up passengers for a trip through snow-covered woods and fields, this Arcade & Attica diesel is an impressive sight. DUNCAN RICHARDS.

During its heyday, the New York Central sent its fast trains racing across New York and onward to Chicago. In rural upstate New York, the NYC ran long freights carrying fruit, coal, lumber, feed, and farm equipment across the Charlotte swing bridge. Some of the same hallowed stretches of track are still in use, and you can ride over them on what is now known as the Ontario-Midland railroad. You have a choice of several railroad journeys beginning near Rochester. Major attractions near this line are the New York Transportation Museum and the Rochester & Genesee Valley Railroad Museum, where you can explore old-fashioned passenger cars, cabooses, milk cars, and eleven other pieces of vintage railroad equipment.

ONTARIO-MIDLAND RAIL EXCURSIONS

WHERE TO BOARD:
Sodus—Take the Maple Street exit of Route 104, travel south one-half mile.

FOR TICKET INFORMATION:
National Railway Historical Society (NRHS), P.O. Box 1161, Webster, NY 14580. Telephone 716-987-1305.

FARES IN 1991:
Adults $9; Children (4–12) $6; Children under 4 ride free. Charters available.

LENGTH OF TRIP:
Fall: Sodus to Newark, NY, 34-mile, 1¾ hour round trip.

DATES OF OPERATION:
Specific Sundays in September and October.

SCHEDULE:
Departures at noon, 2:00 p.m., and 4:00 p.m.

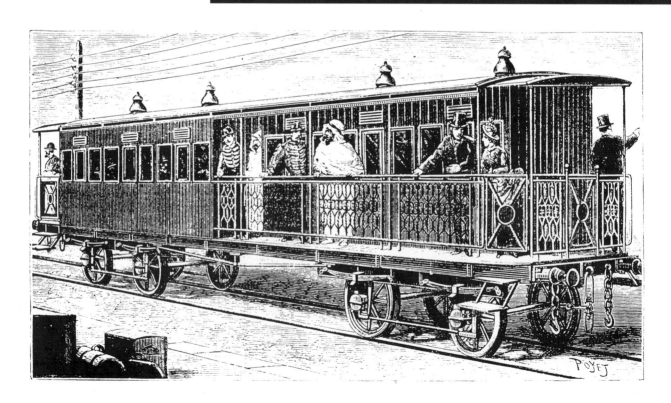

GETTYSBURG RAILROAD

WHERE TO BOARD:
Former Reading Station on Washington Street in Gettysburg.

FOR TICKET INFORMATION:
Gettysburg Railroad, 106 North Washington Street, Gettysburg, PA 17325. Telephone 717-334-6932.

FARES IN 1991:
To Biglerville: Adults $6; Children 3–12 $3.
To Mt. Holly Springs: Adults $15; Children 3–12 $8.
Charter and group rates available.

LENGTH OF TRIP:
Gettysburg to Biglerville, 16-mile 1¼ hour round trip. Gettysburg to Mt. Holly Springs, 50-mile, 5 hour round trip.

DATES OF OPERATION:
April to October.

SCHEDULE:

TO BIGLERVILLE	Weekdays	Thu. & Fri.	Sat. & Sun.
April	—	—	1:00 p.m.
	—	—	3:00 p.m.
May & June	—	10:00 a.m.	1:00 p.m.
	—	12:30 a.m.	3:00 p.m.
July & Aug.	11:00 a.m.	11:00 a.m.	11:00 a.m.
	1:00 p.m.	1:00 p.m.	1:00 p.m.
	—	3:00 p.m.	3:00 p.m.
Sept. & Oct.	—	11:00 a.m.	11:00 a.m
	—	1:00 p.m.	1:00 p.m.
	—	—	3:00 p.m.

Labor Day: 11:00 a.m. & 1:00 p.m.

GETTYSBURG TO MT. HOLLY SPRINGS—Train departs at 10:00 a.m.
September—2nd Saturday
October—1st, 2nd, & 3rd Saturdays and 2nd & 3rd Sundays.

SPECIAL EVENTS:
Train Raid, Lincoln Weekend, Easter Bunny Train, Santa Train, Dinner Trips, Breakfast Trip.

■ The biggest battle ever fought in North America bloodied the fields around this quaint Pennsylvania town. One of the best ways to see the area where this decisive Civil War confrontation took place is by steam train. The Gettysburg Railroad gives you a good look at the wooded hills and farms over which the first day's battle was fought. History is the emphasis here, rather than railroading per se, and it's all a lot of fun. You may want to keep your head down and your hands over your ears when Confederate irregulars hold up the train to search for spies and gold and square off with members of Pennsylvania's 11th Fife and Drum Corps. And don't be surprised if you meet Abraham Lincoln on his way to deliver the Gettysburg Address. Lincoln wrote this brief but immortal speech while riding on a train.

Like many eastern railroads, the Blue Mountain & Reading supplanted a barge canal—in this case the Schuylkill Canal—as a freight and passenger carrier. Originally part of the Pennsylvania Railroad, the BM&R operates sight-seeing tours and carries freight in central Pennsylvania. Among its chief attractions are splendid views of the bucolic Pennsylvania Dutch farm country.

The railroad has been active in restoring vintage rolling stock, depots, and signals so passengers can ride the train right back into the nineteenth century. Ironically, the line also plans to rebuild a portion of the Schuylkill Canal, which it made obsolete long ago. Once the canal restoration is complete, passengers will also be able to ride mule-drawn barges alongside the railroad right of way.

Blue Mountain & Reading Railroad

WHERE TO BOARD:
Temple Station on Tuckerton Road, or South Hamburg Station on Station Road.

FOR TICKET INFORMATION:
Blue Mountain & Reading Railroad, Attention: Passenger Division, P.O. Box 425, Hamburg, PA 19256
Office Phone: (215) 562-4083. Ticket orders only: 1-800-345-7215
Temple Station Phone: (215) 921-1442 South Hamburg Station
Phone: (215) 562-5224 (Stations are open only when trains depart)
Tickets can be purchased at either Temple or Hamburg Stations.

FARES IN 1991:
Adults $7; Children: $5 (ages 3–12 years)
Children under 3 years ride free; Senior Citizens: $6
Season Passes: 60 rides for $75; All Day Passes: $10
Season Passes and Daily Passes are NOT VALID for special events.
No tax on fares.

LENGTH OF TRIP: 26 miles, 1½ hour round trip.

DATES OF OPERATION:
Saturdays and Sundays in May (including Memorial Day), June, September and October. Daily in July and August.
No trains run in November; see Special Events.

SCHEDULE:

	TEMPLE STN. DEPARTURES	S. HAMBURG STN. DEPARTURES
Saturdays and Sundays	1:00 p.m.	Noon
May and June	3:00 p.m.	2:00 p.m.
Including Memorial Day		4:00 p.m.
Daily in July and	1:00 p.m.	Noon
August, through and	3:00 p.m.	2:00 p.m.
including Labor Day		4:00 p.m.
Saturdays and Sundays	1:00 p.m.	Noon
September and October	3:00 p.m.	2:00 p.m.
	4:00 p.m.	

SPECIAL EVENTS:
Easter Bunny Express, Saturday and Sunday on Palm Sunday and Easter Sunday weekends, Children's Weekends: Hobo Weekend on 2nd weekend in June, and Clown Weekend on 4th weekend in August. Fall Foliage Weekends—every weekend in October. Santa Claus Special—Saturdays and Sundays in December, not including weekend before Christmas.

OIL CREEK & TITUSVILLE RAILROAD

WHERE TO BOARD:
Perry Street Station, 409 South Perry St., Titusville. Take Truck Rt. 8 south.
Rynd Farm, 4 miles north of Oil City, off Rt. 8.
Drake Well Museum, south of Titusville off Rt. 8.

FOR TICKET INFORMATION:
OC&T Railroad, P.O. Box 68, Oil City, PA 16301.
Telephone OC&T headquarters 7-days-a-week, 9 a.m.–5 p.m.:
814-676-1733

FARES IN 1992:
Adults $8; Children (3–12) $4; Senior Citizens (60+) $7
Bicycles $1; Canoes $2.
Group Rates available.

LENGTH OF TRIP:
26 miles, 2¹/₂ hour round trip.

DATES OF OPERATION:
Weekends from mid-June through October. Plus Wednesdays in July, August, & October—one round trip departing Perry St. Stn., Titusville, at 1 p.m.

SCHEDULE:

	LEAVE	RETURN
Perry Street	11:45 a.m.	2:15 p.m.
	3:15 p.m.	5:30 p.m.
Drake Well	Noon	2:00 p.m.
	3:30 p.m.	5:15 p.m.
Rynd Farm	1:15 p.m.	4:15 p.m.
	(One Way 4:30 p.m.)	

SPECIAL EVENTS:
Mystery Dinner Excursions; Moonlight Honky Tonk Excursion; Haunted Train Excursion; Santa Train Excursion.

It used to happen every night in just about every small-to-middling-sized town in America. A railroad mail car flashed by and the mail clerk hooked a bag on the fly. Inside the bag was the correspondence of ordinary people—love notes, post cards, business letters, and orders from catalogues. The clerk sorted these important items by lamplight. The mails and rails have enjoyed a long and fruitful marriage. Today, however, the only operating railroad mail car in the United States is on the Oil Creek & Titusville. You can have your stamped letters canceled right on the train.

The OC&T travels past some of America's most important industrial history. For instance, from the train you can see where the world's oil industry began. In 1859 at Oil Creek, Colonel Edwin Drake drilled the first oil well and proved to the world that underground oil could be pumped to the surface in significant quantities. It was also at Oil Creek that the first oil pipeline was constructed to deliver the black liquid gold to trains and barges. And oil money helped pay for foreign arms used by Union troops to win the Civil War.

Just as it does in Texas and Saudi Arabia today, oil made enormous fortunes for some in Pennsylvania. Oil Creek made a tycoon of Jonathan Watson, and the train passes Rynd Farm where he became the world's first oil millionaire. Andrew Carnegie got his start here as well. The oil boom also built up towns. Petroleum Center, Pennsylvania, now a ghost town, mushroomed overnight. Once "busy, bustling, roaring, chaotic, profane and dirty," Oil Creek Valley today has returned to what it was before it sprouted derricks—lovely wooded Pennsylvania farm country. The perfect way to see it is by train.

When the Kinzua Viaduct was built in 1882, it was the highest railroad bridge in the world. At 301 feet, it remains one of the highest even today. Built of iron, the high bridge spans Kinzua Creek on its way to the lumber, coal, and oil country of McKean County, Pennsylvania. Today the bridge is on the National Register of Historic Places. Both steam and diesel sight-seeing trains cross the Kinzua Viaduct and meander through the hills and valleys of the Allegheny National Forest on a thrilling ninety-six-mile round trip railroad journey.

KNOX, KANE, & KINZUA RAILROAD

WHERE TO BOARD:
Depots at Marienville on Rt. 66 in Forest County and at Knox on Rt. 321 South in McKean County.

FOR TICKET INFORMATION:
Knox, Kane, & Kinzua Railroad, P.O. Box 422, Marienville, PA 16239. Telephone: 814-927-6621.

FARES IN 1991:
Marienville to Bridge: Adults $20; Children (3–12) $13
Kane to Bridge: Adults $12.50; Children (3–12) $8
Group rates available.

LENGTH OF TRIP:
Marienville to Kinzua Bridge—96 miles, 8-hour round trip. Kane to Kinzua Bridge—32 miles, 3 1/2-hour round trip.

DATES OF OPERATION:
Weekends in June and September. Tuesday through Sunday in July and August. Wednesday through Sunday 1st two weeks of October. Saturday and Sunday 2nd two weeks in October.

SCHEDULE:
Leave Marienville	8:30 a.m.
Leave Kane	10:45 a.m.
Arrive Kane	2:15 p.m.
Arrive Marienville	4:30 p.m.

STRASBURG RAIL ROAD

WHERE TO BOARD:
Located on Route 741 near Lancaster, Pennsylvania.

FOR TICKET INFORMATION:
Strasburg Rail Road, P.O. Box 96, Strasburg, PA 17579.
Telephone 717-687-7522.

FARES IN 1992:

	Adults	Children
Train	$6	$3
Parlor Car	$8.50	$5

Group rates available.

LENGTH OF TRIP:
Nine miles, 45-minute round trip from Strasburg to Paradise.

DATES OF OPERATION:
Weekends throughout the year; daily mid-March through November. Dinner train runs from the end of March to the end of October by reservation.

SCHEDULE:
Schedule varies with the season. Trains run every half hour in July and August. Complete timetable available upon request.

Strasburg, Pennsylvania, boasts one of America's oldest operating scenic railroads, the Strasburg Rail Road with its four shining Baldwin and Canadian locomotives. A family could easily spend an entire weekend railroading in Strasburg. On the line itself, you can ride to Paradise, Pennsylvania, and back through Lancaster County's rolling Amish country, enjoy dinner in the parlor car "Marion," and explore the historic rolling stock and locomotives on display at the station. Right next door, you can walk through 145 years of railroading history at the Railroad Museum of Pennsylvania. The museum and its extensive yard of rolling stock include more than forty-five locomotives and cars that demonstrate why Pennsylvania was considered the crossroads of rail. There are special events throughout the year and you might like to visit on Circus Weekend in August or take a ride on the Reading Weekend.

Just down the road, the Choo-Choo Barn & Strasburg Train Shop display a 1700-square-foot model of the surrounding countryside and its rail lines. Lovingly constructed by a single family over forty-five years, the layout includes thirteen model trains and 130 animated scenes of Amish country—a three-ring circus, a baseball game, everyday farming and a barn-raising. Anyone who remembers a Lionel train under his or her Christmas tree will also want to visit Strasburg's Toy Train Museum with its extensive collection of toy trains, model layouts, and railroad videos.

In the 1930s the Green Mountain Flyer carried passengers through southern Vermont past some of New England's most beautiful pastoral scenery. It still does. The Flyer's big diesel pulls antique coaches, some dating back to the 1890s. The train courses along the Connecticut River from Bellows Falls to the 1872-vintage depot at Chester, Vermont. Along the way, it passes the waterfalls at Brockways Mills Gorge and crosses a covered railroad bridge where hobos once left messages for one another.

Rugged New England mountains, gorges, and pastureland delight travelers aboard the Green Mountain Flyer. DUNCAN RICHARDS.

GREEN MOUNTAIN RAILROAD

WHERE TO BOARD:
Bellows Falls Station on Depot St. at the junction of the Green Mtn. and Boston & Maine railroads. Take exit 5 or 6 off I-91.

FOR TICKET INFORMATION:
Green Mountain Railroad, P.O. Box 498, Bellows Falls, VT 05101. Telephone: 802-463-3069.

FARES IN 1992:

	Adult	Child (3–12)
Round Trip	$10	$6
One Way	$6	$4

Children under 3 free when held. Group rates available.

LENGTH OF TRIP:
26 miles, 2-hour round trip from Bellows Falls to Chester.

DATES OF OPERATION:
Summer: Tuesdays through Sundays from late June to early September. Closed Mondays except Labor Day.
Fall: Daily mid-Sept. through Columbus Day plus Oct. 17–18.

SCHEDULE:
Summer—June 20–21, & June 27 through Sept. 7.
Fall—Daily Sept. 19-Columbus Day, & weekend of Oct. 17–18.

Depart Bellows Falls—11:00 a.m. & 2:00 p.m.
Depart Chester Depot—12:10 p.m.

SPECIAL EVENTS:
Fall Foliage Specials & Chester Sunset Specials: specific weekends in September and October. Special schedule and fares.

LEGENDS

Railroads were slow to develop down South. By 1861, the industrial North had 22,000 miles of track compared to only 9,000 miles in the rural South—a more than two-to-one advantage. That's one reason the valiant men in gray lost the Civil War. After the war, the imbalance was never corrected, and even today, most of the nation's track mileage lies above the Mason–Dixon line. But if northerners boast more track, southerners lay claim to more *stories* about railroads than anybody.

Storytelling is a southern specialty, like catfish or fried chicken. Some say that spinning out stories and legends comprises the region's chief industry. The South is especially rich in railroading legends, and why not? Trains in general and steam locomotives in particular—with their whistles, speed, and iron muscles—run to the heart of what it is to be an American. Consider the following southern/American folk heroes: John Henry, Casey Jones, and the fleet-footed railroad hound Boomer Sooner.

Railroad Bill, Railroad Bill

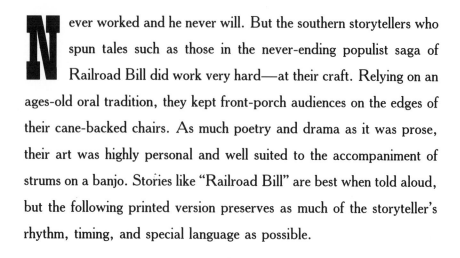

ever worked and he never will. But the southern storytellers who spun tales such as those in the never-ending populist saga of Railroad Bill did work very hard—at their craft. Relying on an ages-old oral tradition, they kept front-porch audiences on the edges of their cane-backed chairs. As much poetry and drama as it was prose, their art was highly personal and well suited to the accompaniment of strums on a banjo. Stories like "Railroad Bill" are best when told aloud, but the following printed version preserves as much of the storyteller's rhythm, timing, and special language as possible.

To folks in Georgia during the Depression it didn't seem like nobody was rich 'cept maybe the railroads. Most folks didn't have much, the rest had less than that, 'specially those who lived in whistlestops like Elewy and Piney Grove. T'was only the railroad steaming through that kept those places alive anyhow. The 10:55 would pause to take on water, leave a passenger or two, and disappear down the tracks. Tramps riding the boxcars would swing down to look for secret marks on houses where they might chop stove wood for a meal or go around back for a pan of cold biscuits. But those marks faded as the Depression deepened. Screen doors slammed in their faces in the summer when the cicadas whirred in the dusty trees, and in the winter poor children huddled in throwed-together shacks along the railroad tracks with only a threadbare quilt between them and the cold. They had nothing a'tall to share with a tramp.

You first heard about Railroad Bill in the barbershop or maybe at the station if you was hanging around waiting for the L&N to steam through. Seems he robbed a train over to Nymph, and the Widow Calloway, she found a whole carton full of canned goods in her shed. Grits there was, and beans, too. Don't seem like he ever come to your town, though. Always the next town. Cans of beans, a warm coat, a sack of coal.

Railroad Bill. The name was whispered at night while the porch swing creaked and a match flared in the darkness. You read about Railroad Bill in the paper and heard it muttered over coffee at Dot's Railroad Café and talked about on the street corners. Then, suddenly, that name was shouted from broadsides plastered all over the depot:

WANTED: Morris Slater

Alias Railroad Bill

For Robbing the Louisville & Nashville Railroad

Reward: $100

For any information

Leading to his Arrest

One hundred dollars. Just you look around these towns—ragged children, out of work tramps and drifters, folks with nothing for supper and the same meal for breakfast. Oh, they'll catch him for sure. Railroad Bill. No one can turn their back on the sound of one hundred dollars.

But they did turn their backs. On a hundred dollars and more.

At night when the L&N whistle floated lonesome through the darkness as the 11:15 rounded the curve by Elewy, you'd lie in your bed and listen to the train go by. Some dark nights there'd be a spit'n of gunfire down by the tracks, and you'd pull the blanket up over your head and hope he'd get away. He was a hero, you see. He was ours, and he

Railroad depots were favorite "observation posts" where townsfolk passed the time of day and watched the comings and goings of both trains and people. BRUCE ROBERTS.

never took nothing for himself. But a man that took sick or was out of work, he'd hear footsteps on the porch, see the shadow of a tall man on the curtain, and find a sack of potatoes or some canned goods for his children by the door. Come morning the little ones would gather empty boxes and crates along the railroad tracks.

It got so folks would say they couldn't catch him. Turned himself into a hound and run away through the woods when the sheriff come after him. One hundred dollars waiting, but no one to turn him in. No one to collect that big reward. When the sheriff came knocking at the door, no one knew nothing about ol' Railroad Bill. Never even heard of the man.

Just the Widow Calloway. She knew. A can of beans clutched in her old hands, she'd whisper, "Bless you, Railroad Bill," and silently she'd close the screen door.

A Southern freight car, no longer in use by either railroad or hobo, rests on a side track. BRUCE ROBERTS.

A Steel-Driving Man

Folks say jagged forks of lightning split the sky over Tennessee and the Mississippi River reversed course and ran north for a thousand miles the night John Henry was born. Everyone could see this was no ordinary baby. He was not even a day old and already "he had a deep voice, like a preacher man," his mama claimed. His daddy was proud to see his son had shoulders "like an Alabama mule." They say John Henry finished his first meal and then went out to look for work. Because of his great strength, he became a steel-driving man.

Like most hard-working heroes, John Henry had a touch of the rogue in him, a big mouth, a way with the women, and more stories told about him than he had hairs on his head. It is said he could pick more cotton, lay more track, and build more bridges than anyone. But he was best at driving steel—the back-breaking job of crushing rock during railroad grade and tunnel construction.

In 1870 the Chesapeake & Ohio Railroad began laying tracks in West Virginia. At a place called the Big Bend on the Potomac River, a formidable mountain blocked the right of way. There was no going around it or over it. The only way to get by was to bore a tunnel right through the iron-hard rock. It was a big job, big enough even for a steel-driving man the likes of John Henry. "I'm a man who can whip steel down," John Henry said when he signed on. And sure enough, he proved as good as his word. He could work all day and into the night wielding two twenty-pound hammers to drill and smash through the rock and carve out the tunnel.

Then a rival construction company started work at the opposite end of the tunnel, on the other side of the mountain. Having no John Henry on their team, the rival crew employed one of the newfangled mechanical drills powered—like a locomotive—by steam. Soon a race was on to see which of the two crews could dig the fastest, and after a lot of bragging and boasting (and a few fist fights) the race boiled down to just one man against the machine.

The man who would challenge the machine was, of course, John

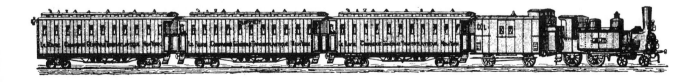

In the lovely West Virginia countryside, a Cass Scenic Railroad train pauses and puffs while waiting for another train to pass. BRUCE ROBERTS.

Henry. His fellow workers all agreed that he was their champion. "I can drive from both shoulders myself," said a fellow steel driver. "But I'm as far behind John Henry as the moon is behind the sun. Let him take on the steam drill." Said another, "John Henry could take that hammer between his teeth and drive with his hands tied behind his back and still beat that steam drill."

John Henry, too, knew he was the man for the job. "Excuse me for laughing, Captain," he told his foreman. "I've burned out all the men you got, and I can burn out that steam drill."

The race was arranged and bets were laid. John Henry's backers offered him $100 if he could do as he had said and sink more steel than the steam-powered drill. On the appointed day a throng of workers gathered around. Being men of muscle and bone—and not of iron—themselves, most had bet their hard-earned money on John Henry. "Do it, John, do it!" they shouted. "Wop that steel on down."

Stripped to the waist and with two new twenty-pound hammers in his hands, John Henry stood ready. The timekeeper gave the signal, and man and machine pounded away at steel and stone. Thirty minutes later, the timekeeper yelled, "Time!" and it was all over. Everyone ran to see what had happened. John Henry had driven two holes seven feet into the mountain; the steam drill had driven only one.

John Henry had won, but the effort had broken his big heart. He went home after the race feeling poorly and by morning he was dead. When he was buried, people came from all over to say good-bye to the man who had beaten a machine. His wife had engraved on his tombstone: "Here lies a steel-driving man."

Even after John Henry was gone, folks said you could still hear his hammer ringing through the West Virginia mountains. When workers heard that sound, they laid down their hammers to listen. All during the 1870s and '80s there were work stoppages on the C&O, and the railroad never managed to recruit local men to work on the line where John Henry "laid down his hammer and died."

A sleek and shiny diesel awaits riders on the Western Maryland Scenic Railroad. PHOTO BY TIM WILSON; COURTESY WESTERN MARYLAND SCENIC RAILROAD, CUMBERLAND, MARYLAND.

Boomer Sooner Hound

W hen railroads became firmly established with sturdy tracks and reliable engines, schedules became all-important; engineers and crew were ruled by the large silver watches they carried in their pockets. The trains ran so regularly that local people used them for clocks. They were even referred to by their times—the 12:55 or the 9:15. If a train fell behind schedule, the engineer would use the raw power and speed of the locomotive to make up the lost time. However, as the following (very tall) tale makes clear, the big locomotives were not always the fastest "critters" on the tracks.

A Boomer fireman is never long for any one road. One year he may be working on the B&O and the next he's heaving black diamonds for the Katy or the Wabash. He goes wherever there's a boom, and when it busts, he moves on. He travels light and travels far and doesn't let any grass grow under his feet when they get to itching for the greener pastures

A pair of puffer-bellies wait side by side for their next group of passengers.
PHOTO BY LARRY BELCHER; COURTESY CASS SCENIC RAILROAD, CASS, WEST VIRGINIA.

on the next road or the next division, or maybe to hell and gone on the other side of the mountains. He doesn't need furniture and he doesn't need many clothes, and God knows he doesn't need a family or a dog.

But this particular Boomer, he had a dog all right. When the Boomer pulled into the road master's office looking for a job, there was that "sooner" hound of his loping after him. That hound would sooner run than eat and he'd sooner eat than fight or do something useful like catch a rabbit. Not that a rabbit would have any chance if the sooner really wanted to nail him, but that crazy hound-dog didn't like to do anything but run and he was the fastest thing on four legs.

"I might use you," said the road master. "Can you get a boarding place for the dog?"

"Oh, he goes along with me," the Boomer replied. "I raised him from a pup and he ain't never spent a night or a day or even an hour far away from me. He'd cry like his poor heart would break and raise such a ruckus nobody couldn't sleep, eat, or hear themselves think for miles about."

"Well, I don't see how that would work out," the road master said. "It's against the rules of the road to allow a passenger in the cab, man or beast. You look like a man that could keep a boiler popping off on an uphill grade, but I just don't see how we could work it if the hound won't listen to reason while you're on your runs."

"Why, he ain't no trouble," said the Boomer. "He just runs alongside, and when I'm on a freight run he chases around a little in the fields to pass the time away."

"Don't spread that bull around here."

"He'll do it without half trying," the Boomer went on. "It's a little bit tiresome on him having to travel at such a slow gait, but that sooner would do anything to stay close by me. He loves me that much."

"Go spread that on the grass to make it green," said the road master in disgust.

Red lanterns and mechanical switches symbolize our railroading past. DUNCAN RICHARDS.

Exhileration mixes with regret as you disembark from a scenic train ride. BRUCE ROBERTS.

"I'll lay my first paycheck against a fiver that he'll be as fresh as a daisy and his tongue behind his teeth when we pull into the junction. Why he'll run around the station a hundred times or so just to limber up."

"It's a bet," said the road master.

On the first run, the sooner moved in what was a slow walk for him. He kept looking up into the cab where the Boomer was shoveling in the coal.

"He looks worried," said the Boomer. "He thinks overtime is going to catch us, we're making such bad time."

The road master was so sore at losing the bet that he transferred the Boomer to a local passenger run and doubled the stakes. The sooner speeded up to a slow trot, but he had to kill a lot of time at that, not to get too far ahead of the engine.

Then the road master got mad enough to bite off a drawbar. People got to watching the sooner trotting alongside the train and began thinking it must be a mighty slow road. Passengers might as well walk; they'd get there just as fast. And if you shipped a yearling calf to market, it'd be a bologna bull before it reached the stockyards. Of course, the trains were keeping up their schedules the same as usual, but that's the way it looked to people who saw a no-good mangy sooner hound beating all the trains without his tongue hanging out an inch or letting out the least little pant.

It was giving the road a black eye, all right. The road master would have fired the Boomer and told him to hit the grit with his sooner and never come back again, but he was stubborn from the word "go" and hated worse than anything to own up he was licked.

"I'll fix that sooner," thought the road master. "I'll slap the Boomer into the cab of the Cannonball, and if anything on four legs can keep up with the fastest thing on wheels, I'd admire to see it. That sooner'll be left so far behind it'll take nine dollars to send him a post card."

The word got around that the sooner was going to try to keep up with the Cannonball. Farmers left off plowing, hitched up, and drove to the right of way to see the sight. It was like a circus day or the county fair. The schools dismissed the pupils, and not a mill could keep enough men to bother heating up the boilers.

The road master got right in the cab so the Boomer couldn't ease off on the job to let the sooner keep up. A clear track south for a hundred miles was ordered for the Cannonball, and all the switches were spiked down until after that streak of lightning had passed. It took three men to see the Cannonball on that run—one to say "There she comes," another to say "There she is," and one more to say "There she goes." You couldn't see a thing for steam, cinders, and smoke, and the rails sang like a violin for a half hour after she'd passed into the next county.

Every valve was popping off, and the wheels were flying along three feet in the air above the roadbed. But the Boomer wasn't worried a bit. He was so sure the sooner would keep up that he wore the hinges right off the fire door and fifteen pounds of him melted off and ran right down into his shoes.

The road master stuck his head out the cab window, and—whoosh!—off went his hat and almost his head. The suction like to have jerked his arms from their sockets as he took hold of the window seat.

It was all he could do to see, and gravel pinged against his goggles like hailstones, but he let out a whoop of joy.

"The sooner! The sooner!" he yelled. "He's gone! He's gone for true! Ain't nowhere in sight!"

"I can't understand that," hollered the Boomer. "He ain't never laid down on me yet. It just ain't like him to lay down on me. Leave me take a peek."

He dropped his shovel and poked out his head. Then he whooped even louder than the road master had.

"He's true blue as they come!" the Boomer shouted. "Got the interests of the company at heart, too. He's still with us."

"Where do you get that stuff?" asked the road master. "I don't see him nowhere. Not hide nor hair of him."

"We're going so fast the journal boxes are on fire and melting the axles like hot butter," the Boomer answered. "The sooner's running up and down the train hoisting a leg above the boxes doing his level best to put out some of the fires. That dog is true blue as they come. He's the fastest thing on four legs, but he's only using three of them now."

The story of the "Boomer Sooner Hound" is told in numerous versions in both the South and Midwest. This one is based on a telling by Jack Conroy published in "Chicago Industrial Folklore," a manuscript of the Depression-era Federal Writers' Project.

Modern diesel engines often sport distinctive paint jobs, much as their steam predecessors showed off with polished brass. BRUCE ROBERTS.

Scalded to Death by Steam

Come all you rounders, I want you to hear
The story told of a brave engineer.
Old Casey Jones was the rounder's name;
On a six-eight wheeler he won his fame.

WALLACE SAUNDERS

Stories such as those about Railroad Bill, John Henry, and certainly the Boomer Sooner Hound require a stretch of the imagination—something students of literature call a "willing suspension of disbelief." But many folk tales and folk heroes are based on real events and real people. For instance, Casey Jones was, in fact, a railroad engineer, and just as legend has it, he drove a train known as the Cannonball Express. Nearly everyone has heard of Casey, and it's hard not to imagine him bound for glory on his thundering locomotive. Actually, Casey's name was not really "Casey" but John Luther Jones, and he was, perhaps, a bit less of a hero than he was a reckless driver. In legend, however, and in the hearts of music lovers everywhere, he will always be remembered as Casey Jones, the brave engineer who died blowing the whistle of his locomotive to warn his passengers of imminent disaster.

The accident that took engineer Jones' life was, unfortunately, not all that unusual. It was a disaster of a type repeated hundreds of times on tracks from Montana to Mississippi, Maine to California: A speeding train slams into the back of another train either stopped or moving along slowly on the same track.

Early on the morning of April 30, 1900, Jones was roaring south on the line from Memphis to New Orleans, pushing his locomotive to the limit trying to make up time he had lost earlier. Suddenly, in the tunnel-like darkness ahead, two red lights loomed—from the caboose of a sidetracked freight train. Jones had only an instant to apply the brakes and blow his whistle. Then he entered the realm of legend.

More than a few engineers have lost their lives as he did, ramming the back of a parked train, but Jones' death made him the most famous railroad engineer in history. Why? Because of a song.

It was Wally Saunders, an illiterate laborer in the Cannonball Roundhouse, who brought Casey his fame. Saunders liked to sing while he worked, and he made up ballads to help pass the time. You can hear the rhythm of his work in his ballad about Casey Jones—suggestions of the heavy strokes needed to swab down engines or the sweep of a man's shoulders when shoveling coal. The ballad recounts the tragic loss of a man (Casey Jones) and a locomotive (old No. 382) that Saunders knew well. In retelling the story of the crash, however, Saunders took some liberties with the truth. But so do all poets, and although he could neither read nor write, that's just what Saunders was—a poet. Something in his ballad touched the human spirit. For that reason and because it was a lot of fun to sing, Saunders' ballad was soon heard in music halls all across the country, and before long, the name Casey Jones had been permanently chiseled into the stone of American myth.

What really happened on the Cannonball Express that spring morning? According to Sim Webb, Casey's fireman, the Express was indeed running late. The train had more than an hour to make up on the run from Memphis to New Orleans. To get back "on the advertised" Casey pushed every ounce of steam he could get into old No. 382. The Express really was a cannonball that morning.

Tragedy lay waiting near Vaughn, Mississippi, at a treacherous double-S curve in the tracks. It had been raining at Vaughn, and the

Careful maintenance is essential to a safe trip. At top, a worker squirts oil on a wheel; at bottom, a man double-checks a connection. BRUCE ROBERTS PHOTOS.

clouds hung down heavily almost to track level. Fireman Sim was peering down the line through the murk when he saw the red warning lights on the back of a caboose. "Look out, Mr. Casey!" Sim yelled. "We're going to ram somethin'!"

The engineer kicked aside his seat and, too late, threw on the brakes. "Jump, Sim!" he shouted. Sim swung out from the engine and hit the ground hard. The impact knocked him out. When Sim came to, the big fourteen-wheeler lay on its side in a ditch, steam hissing from a dozen ruptures. Men came running with lanterns and found Casey's crushed and scalded body in the wreckage, the rope pull from his famous whistle still clutched in his hand. The Cannonball Express had smashed right through the caboose and two freight cars loaded with corn and hay. The Cannonball's coal car lay sideways across the track and the mail car had been pushed on top of the water car, but miraculously, no one but Casey was seriously hurt.

Whose fault was the accident? The freight train had pulled onto a siding to make room for the Cannonball and left several of its cars jutting out onto the main track. What was worse, the freight had no flagman at the rear to warn an approaching train of danger. But Casey was also to blame. As the ballad makes clear, he was pushing his old locomotive much too fast.

However, the ballad asks no questions about who was at fault, and neither does the legend. There are better ways to remember railroad heroes. A bronze tablet honors Casey in Cayce, Kentucky, the town that gave him his nickname. Perhaps a more fitting memorial is the field of wild corn that still grows beside that dangerous S curve in the tracks near Vaughn, Mississippi. The corn was first scattered here in April of 1900 when a freight car loaded with corn was rammed by the Illinois Central Fast Mail Train No. 1—the Cannonball Express. But the best way of all to remember is Wally Saunders' song, which reminds us that all railroaders have a little of Casey in them.

Tales that are earnest, noble and grand
Are all in the life of a railroad man.

READER RAILROAD

WHERE TO BOARD:
Adam's Crossing Station—located between Camden and Prescott on Highway 368 just off Arkansas Highway 24. (General offices are located in Hot Springs; no trains operate from Hot Springs area.)

FOR TICKET INFORMATION:
Reader Railroad, P.O. Box 507, Hot Springs, AR 71902.
Telephone: 501-624-6881.

FARES IN 1991:
Adults $6; Children (4–11) $3.60
Children under 4 ride free with parent.
Group rates available. Fares may be slightly higher for special events.

LENGTH OF TRIP:
6 miles, 1 hour and 40 minute round trip between Adams Crossing and Camp DeWoody.

DATES OF OPERATION:
Weekends and holidays from the first Saturday in May to the end of October.

SCHEDULE:
Depart Adams Crossing
Saturdays—11:00 a.m. & 2:00 p.m.
Sundays—2:00 p.m.

SPECIAL EVENTS:
Most holiday weekends—call for info.

■ Like many short-line railroads, the Reader got its start in the lumbering trade. Originally a narrow-gauge line, it meandered through bottomlands and climbed up along tumbling creeks to haul out the virgin timber harvested in the highlands of central Arkansas. Eventually, the Reader was converted to standard gauge. In fact, it is among the oldest common-carrier lines in the U.S. still using steam and still operating on standard-gauge tracks.

The line features three vintage locomotives with boilers fired by oil or wood. They haul antique passenger cars heated by wood stoves and lighted with kerosene lamps. Passengers enjoy dogwood and azaleas in the spring and a vibrant splash of fall color in autumn. One of the most interesting parts of a trip on the so-called "Possum Trot Line" is the process of turning around for the return trip: a hand-operated turntable reverses the direction of the locomotive while the passenger cars and caboose wait on a sidetrack.

True to its promise, the Bluegrass Railroad carries passengers into the heart of scenic Bluegrass country. The ninety-minute ride over the old Louisville Southern Mainline begins at Woodford County Park and rumbles out over rolling hills covered with the lush carpet of grass that gives the region its name. During most warm-weather months, wildflowers spangle the grass with color.

Along the way, white fences line pastures inhabited by some of the most aristocratic thoroughbreds in America—after all, this is the land God had in mind when he created the horse. You'll also see tobacco farms; the broad-leafed plants are lovely even if you object to their use.

A trestle, soaring 240 feet above wild and rugged Lock Hollow, offers a breathtaking view. So do the limestone cuts where the Kentucky River has sliced down through eons of prehistory. But the best sight-seeing waits at Young's High Bridge in Tyronne. Built in 1889 to span the Kentucky River canyon, the bridge is 281 feet high and 1659 feet long.

BLUEGRASS RAILROAD

WHERE TO BOARD:
Woodford County Park, US 62 west of Versailles.

FOR TICKET INFORMATION:
Bluegrass Railroad Museum, P.O. Box 27, Versailles, KY 40383. Telephone: 606-873-2476 or 1-800-755-2476.

FARES IN 1991:
Adults $6; Senior Citizens (62 & over) $5; Children (3–12 yrs. old) $4. Children under 3 ride free.
Group rates available.

LENGTH OF TRIP:
11 miles, 1½ hour round trip.

DATES OF OPERATION:
Weekends May through October.

SCHEDULE:
Saturdays—10:00 a.m., 1:00 p.m. & 4:00 p.m.
Sundays—1:00 p.m. & 4:00 p.m.

SPECIAL EVENTS:
Lady Gangster Train Robbery, Ice Cream Special, Clown Days, Civil War Re-enactment & Train Robbery, Hobo Lunch Train, The Thoroughbred Limited, Fall Foliage, Halloween Ghost Train, Santa Claus Special.

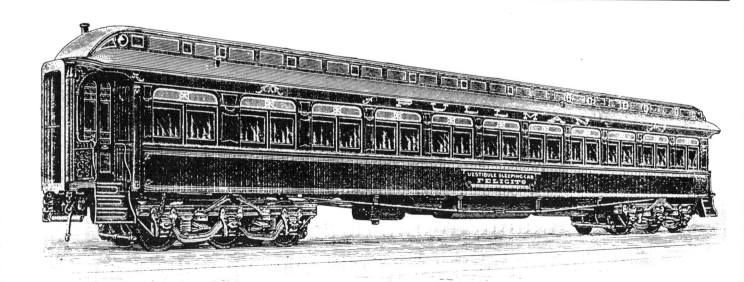

WESTERN MARYLAND SCENIC RAILROAD

WHERE TO BOARD:
Western Maryland Station in Cumberland—From I-68, take Downtown Cumberland Exit 43C; follow signs for tourist information.

FOR TICKET INFORMATION:
Western Maryland Scenic Railroad, Western Maryland Station, Cumberland, MD 21502. Telephone 301-759-4400, or 1-800-TRAIN-50.

FARES IN 1992:

	May-Sept. Nov. & Dec.	October
Adults	$13.00	$15.50
Senior (60+ yrs. old)	11.50	$15.00
Children (2–12 yrs. old)	8.00	9.00
One Way	11.00	14.50

Group rates available. Children under 2, not occupying a seat, ride free.

LENGTH OF TRIP:
32 miles round trip, 45 minutes each way with 90-minute layover in Frostburg.

DATES OF OPERATION:
May through early December.

SCHEDULE:

Month	Tues.–Fri.	Sat. & Sun.
May	11:30 a.m.	11:30 a.m.
		—
June through Sept.	11:30 a.m.	11:30 a.m.
		3:30 p.m.
October	11:30 a.m.	11:30 a.m.
		3:30 p.m.
November	—	11:30 a.m.

All times are departing from Cumberland.

SPECIAL EVENTS:
Memorial Day, Labor Day, Halloween Special, Santa's Express.

Two handsome diesel locomotives emblazoned with the yellow fireball of the "Fast Freight Herald" head up the Western Maryland train as it leaves Cumberland and plunges into the Alleghenies. On tracks laid by the venerable B&O line, the train rounds legendary Helmstetter Horseshoe Curve and chugs through the 914-foot Brush Tunnel. Climbing 1300 feet over Piney Mountain, it passes the town of Mt. Savage where the first T-shaped iron rails were manufactured. After crossing an old steel girder bridge, it steams into Frostburg where a turntable reverses the engine for the return trip. A ninety-minute layover at Frostburg allows passengers to enjoy the depot shops and restaurant.

Reversing direction for the return trip, the Western Maryland diesel rides a vintage turntable at the Frostburg depot. PHOTO BY TIM WILSON; COURTESY WESTERN MARYLAND SCENIC RAILROAD.

■ Over fifty years ago, as our country was recovering from the Great Depression and facing the spectre of World War II, short-line passenger and freight trains chugged from whistle stop to whistle stop, linking small towns across America. The Tennessee Valley Railroad recreates this 1930s feeling right down to the Burma Shave signs. Locomotive crews wear overalls, bandannas, and gauntlet gloves, and carry pocket watches with suitably long chains; a conductor in full uniform punches each ticket with a unique railroad punch. Tickets are copies of those issued by the Georgia Railroad in 1932. Passengers board matching restored coaches sporting maroon livery and gold striping, and the train doesn't move until the conductor gives his "All abooooard!"

TENNESSEE VALLEY RAILROAD

WHERE TO BOARD:
Grand Junction Station, Cromwell Rd., or East Chattanooga Depot and Shop, North Chamberlain. Call for detailed directions, if needed.

FOR TICKET INFORMATION:
Tennessee Valley Railroad, 4119 Cromwell Road, Chattanooga, TN 37421. Telephone 615-894-8028.

FARES IN 1992:
E. Chatta. to Grd. Junct.—Adults $6.75; Children (3–12) $3.25. Downtown Arrow (Connecting service from E. Chatta. to Chatta. Choo Choo Hotel Complex)—Adults $11; Children (3–12) $7.50. Group rates available.

LENGTH OF TRIP:
6 miles, 45-minute round trip, plus audio visual show & display.

SCHEDULE:
Depots open 30 min. before first train & close 15 min. after last train.

Train No.	E. Chatta.	Grd. Junct.
A1	#LV 9:30 a.m.	LV 10:00 a.m.
1	*#LV 10:20 a.m.	LV 10:45 a.m.
2	*#LV 11:25 a.m.	LV 11:40 a.m.
3	*LV 12:15 p.m.	LV 12:40 p.m.
4	LV 1:15 p.m.	LV 1:40 p.m.
5	LV 2:15 p.m.	LV 2:40 p.m.
6	LV 3:15 p.m.	LV 3:40 p.m.
7	LV 4:15 p.m.	**LV 4:55 p.m.

DOWNTOWN ARROW—Service to Chattanooga Choo Choo.

Train No.	E. Chatta.	Grd. Junct.	Chatta. Choo Choo
21	LV 11:25 a.m.	##LV 11:50 a.m.	AR 12:50 p.m.
22		AR 2:15 p.m.	LV 1:20 p.m.
22		LV 2:30 p.m.	
22	AR 2:45 p.m.		

Switching & engine change at E. Chattanooga if required.

23	LV 3:05 p.m.		AR 3:55 p.m.
24	AR 4:55 p.m.		LV 4:00 p.m.
24	AR 5:20 p.m.	**LV 5:05 p.m.	

* Trains 1, 2, 3 or school charters only run daily in May.   # Does not run on Sunday.
** Does not pick up at Grand Junction.
** Stops at E. Chatta. Sundays or on demand on other days.

SPECIAL EVENTS:
Tennessee Autumn Specials in October. Other Mainline trips TBA.

Texas State Railroad

WHERE TO BOARD:
Rusk Depot—in Rusk Park, 2.5 miles west of Rusk on US 84.
Palestine Depot—3 miles east of Palestine on US 84.

FOR TICKET INFORMATION:
Texas State Railroad, P.O. Box 39, Rusk TX 75785. Telephone
903-683-2561, or in Texas only 1-800-442-8951.

FARES IN 1991:
One Way—Adults $8; Children (3–12) $4
Round Trip—Adults $11; Children (3–12) $6.

LENGTH OF TRIP:
50 miles, 4 hour round trip between Rusk and Palestine.

DATES OF OPERATION:
Saturdays & Sundays, March 21–May 24.
Thursdays through Mondays, May 25–August 16.
Saturdays & Sundays, August 22–November 1, plus Labor Day.

SCHEDULE:
Rusk Train

LV Rusk Depot	11:00 a.m.
AR Palestine Depot	12:30 p.m.
LV Palestine Depot	1:30 p.m.
AR Rusk Depot	3:00 p.m.

Palestine Train

LV Palestine Depot	11:00 a.m.
AR Rusk Depot	12:30 p.m.
LV Rusk Depot	1:30 p.m.
AR Palestine Depot	3:00 p.m.

■ Shivers run up and down your spine as the train whistle echoes through the East Texas Piney Woods near Rusk and Palestine, Texas. With a whoosh of steam and the special call only a steam whistle can issue, three veteran steam locomotives pull scarlet, gold, and black coaches over twenty-five miles of track from the Victorian depot at Palestine to the stone depot at Rusk. Originally built by inmates of the East Texas Penitentiary, the Texas State Railroad was run by prisoners to haul wood and iron ore to the prison smelter. Eventually the line hooked up with the Cotton Belt Line and the Union Pacific to become part of the network of railroads in East Texas.

Ready to roll, an engineer climbs aboard the Texas State Railroad.
COURTESY TEXAS STATE RAILROAD.

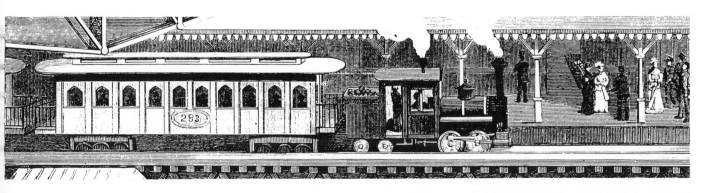

On the second level of the switchback, the small Shay engine shudders to a halt. The cab is silent save for the water in the boiler, the pounding of the pump, and the roaring coal in the firebox. Red McMillion, the engineer, opens the throttle and lets loose two shrill blasts on the steam whistle. The engine shakes itself and begins again to push six cars along the switchback. Ahead, a steep grade leads the train up a mountain.

Climbing the second switchback the Shay begins to roar. The engine really pushes, slows for a moment, and then emerges into warm sunlight from the cool dark of the forest. More than six hundred feet below, passengers can see green meadows with grazing cows, the Greenbrier River Valley, and the stacks of the old lumber mill at Cass.

The engine labors. The engineer turns with a grin, "She's right up to her knees against the mountain." But the Shay does what it was built to do—pushes the cars slowly and steadily around 22° curves and up a nine percent grade, snaking through forests and around hills. Ahead the arch of Whittaker Station comes into sight. Slowly the train eases into it.

In Cass today people see coal smoke rising and live with the sounds of blowing whistles and ringing bells just as they did eighty years ago. Geared locomotives climb mountains steeped in logging and railroad tradition. Passengers of the Cass Scenic Railroad can experience these historical riches firsthand.

CASS SCENIC RAILROAD

WHERE TO BOARD:
Depot in downtown Cass.

FOR TICKET INFORMATION:
Cass Scenic Railroad, P.O. Box 107, Cass, WV 24927. Telephone 304-456-4300; 1-800-CALL-WVA.

FARES IN 1991:
To Bald Knob—Adults $11; Children $5.
To Whittaker Station—Adults $8; Children $4.
Dinner Train—Adults $22; Children $15.
Charter rates available.

LENGTH OF TRIP:
To Bald Knob—22 mile, 4½ hour round trip.
To Whittaker Station—8 mile, 1½ hour round trip.

DATES OF OPERATION:
May to last weekend in October.

SCHEDULE:
Bald Knob—Tuesday–Sunday, leaves at noon.
Whittaker—Daily, 11:00 a.m., 1:00 p.m. & 3:00 p.m.
Dinner Train—Reservations required. Call for information.

SPECIAL EVENTS:
Halloween Train, Railfan Weekend.

In autumn, a ride on the Cass is a colorful experience. PHOTO BY STEPHEN J. SHALUTA, JR.; COURTESY CASS SCENIC RAILROAD.

THE MIDWEST

DISASTERS

The Midwest is the heartland of railroading in America. From the economic and cultural hub of Chicago, railroad lines radiate in all directions like the spokes of an enormous wheel—except, of course, into Lake Michigan. In fact, it was Great Lakes shipping that turned Chicago and other lakeside towns into magnets for trade, and the railroads extended the push and pull of that commerce to every city and town in the region.

But the influence of railroads on the Midwest goes far beyond their economic importance. The rails are inextricably woven into the fabric of midwestern culture. Every locomotive and every railroader have their own stories to tell in this land of heroes, hobos, farmers, and capitalists, of isolated depots surrounded by endless fields of wheat and corn, and of speeding mail trains whistling in the night.

Robin Hood of Rails

Earlier a key to commerce in the Midwest, railroads today carry curious and nostalgic passengers with a taste for the past. PHOTO BY SKIP GATERMANN; COURTESY ST. LOUIS, IRON MOUNTAIN & SOUTHERN RAILROAD, JACKSON, MISSOURI.

Among the most storied and notorious midwesterners of all time was a man who made his living robbing trains—and an occasional bank. Maybe it was his clear blue eyes or his small white hands; maybe it was because his father was a Baptist minister. Or maybe it was because he and his brother Frank took such good care of their mother, but Jesse James impressed people as a kindly man . . . at least until he pulled his gun. To poor farmers, desperate for a hero in the hard, monopolistic times following the Civil War, he was a midwestern Robin Hood at war with capitalist scoundrels and money-grubbing railroads. But to those who care to check the facts, he was also a cold-blooded killer. As is usually the case, the facts and the legend do not entirely agree.

Jesse James saw himself more as a southerner than a midwesterner, more as a Rebel than a Robin Hood. He and his brother Frank fought with William Quantrill's irregulars along the Kansas–Missouri border during the Civil War. When the South was defeated, they came home bitter, restless, and ready to pitch in with the general lawlessness that seized southern Missouri following the war. In 1866 a dozen men, including James, rode into Liberty, Missouri, and pulled off America's first daylight bank robbery. Three years later at Gallatin, Missouri, a bank was robbed and a horse left behind identified as "belonging to a young man named James." Jesse and Frank James made the newspapers regularly from then on, robbing banks—and later trains—all over the central United States.

Some say it was Jesse's friend and fellow bandit Cole Younger who first suggested robbing trains—as a way to strike back at greedy northern industrialists. But the James brothers got credit—or discredit—for

the idea. Jesse James seemed to revel in publicity and may have taken an active hand in building his own legend. By the time his thirteen-year career as an outlaw was ended by a bullet in the back (fired not by a lawman but by a member of his own gang), he had become a giant in the minds of many, if not most, Americans.

One of the James brothers' earliest attempts at train robbery took place on the Iron Mountain Railroad in the Missouri Ozarks. The Iron Mountain line (see page 63) recreates this robbery several times each summer so visitors can share the excitement.

In the winter of 1874, newspaper headlines blared "James Gang Robs Iron Mountain—Most Daring Robbery on Record." Readers found the story of the robbery thrilling. It seemed the James Gang had "robbed the 5:04 Little Rock Express taking $3,000 and escaped without a trace. The notorious outlaws entered Gads Hill, 100 miles south of St. Louis, on horseback and quickly took over the little town which is scarcely more than a way station for the St. Louis, Iron Mountain & Southern Railway. . . . According to witnesses, the gang surrounded the tiny depot and captured the station agent, the village doctor and his son, the blacksmith and several townspeople who were waiting to watch the daily express pass by. Guns drawn, the desperados locked the good citizens of Gads Hill in the station office and flagged the 5:04 which does not make a regular stop at Gads Hill. After robbing the

St. Louis, Iron Mountain & Southern passengers are treated to an exciting reenactment of the James gang robbery—in the midst of tranquil Missouri scenery. PHOTO BY SKIP GATERMANN; COURTESY ST. LOUIS, IRON MOUNTAIN & SOUTHERN RAILROAD.

passengers, the gang took $1,000 from the express car and $2,000 from the mail."

When the train began to move again after the robbery, Jesse James rode alongside the engine and handed the engineer a piece of paper. "Give this to the newspapers," he said. "We like to do things in style." The paper contained a press release with the headline, "The Most Daring Train Robbery on Record." Several years later, Mrs. Jesse James confided to the press that the proceeds of the Gads Hill robbery paid for their honeymoon in Texas.

With a price on his head, Jesse James had plenty of bounty hunters on his tail, but none of them ever caught him. James especially enjoyed taunting the agents sent after him and his gang by the Pinkerton Agency. One of these was D.T. Bligh, a particularly tenacious Pinkerton agent. With no photographs or portraits of the James brothers, Bligh began a careful study of their daily habits, hoping to identify them that way. Bligh read dozens of newspaper accounts and interviewed anyone he could who knew anything about the Jameses. What he discovered was disappointing: They had no settled habits since they were always on the run. In fact, they used the very trains they robbed to move from place to place.

While Bligh was learning practically nothing about the Jameses, they were learning more than a little about him. Frank and Jesse made a policy of finding out all they could about their pursuers, and they soon identified Bligh.

One day in St. Louis, Jesse James spotted Bligh, who by that time was hot on his trail. Never at a loss for audacity, the outlaw struck up a conversation with the Pinkerton man and even invited him to have a drink at the railroad depot. James introduced himself as an agent for a tombstone company. Bligh confided that he was a Pinkerton agent on the trail of the notorious Jesse James. The day was hot, the job was lonely, and perhaps the drink had loosened Bligh's tongue. "Gee," he said, "I'd sure like to see Jesse James before I die." The conversation then turned to other topics, and James finally said good-bye and boarded his train.

A few days later Bligh received a post card reminding him of the drink he had in St. Louis. "You have seen Jesse James," said the card. "Now you can go ahead and die. Your friend, Jesse James."

Train robberies make exciting newspaper copy, but so do major disasters. In the summer of 1894, headlines blazed with news of one of the most spectacular conflagrations in the nation's history. Fire had consumed an entire town—and much of the surrounding countryside as well—in northern Minnesota. Except for a pair of locomotives and their brave crews, the calamity might have been much worse.

The summer of 1894 was one of the driest on record in Minnesota. By the end of August, the woods around the small town of Hinckley had become a great pile of kindling waiting for a match to turn them into an inferno. Then, somewhere out in the forest, the inevitable happened—a fire started. Like so many forest fires, no one knows how this one began. Perhaps a carelessly banked campfire provided the spark, or maybe lightning touched it off, but on September 1, folks in Hinckley looked up and saw a column of fire rising over the woods to the south of town. They could smell charcoal and even taste it. The air grew heavy with haze and turned the daylight to a sickly green. The smoke got so thick it eventually blotted out the sun, and chickens went to roost at noon.

For a while it seemed the fire might burn itself out before reaching

Train Ride into Hell

A well-kept caboose brings up the rear in style on the Nicolet Scenic line.
COURTESY NICOLET SCENIC RAILROAD, LAONA, WISCONSIN.

Hinckley, but then the wind came up. Suddenly, trees just at the edge of town bloomed orange with flame. Buildings in town, their wooden walls parched by the summer heat, burst into flames. The heat was so terrific that canned goods in the general stores exploded. The fire was feeding on itself, producing its own winds in a process sometimes called a firestorm. The town was doomed, and its people could only hope to get out alive. But that would not be easy: they were encircled by towers of flame.

At the Hinckley depot two trains from the Lake Superior & Mississippi Railroad sat ready to roll. The engineers, Best and Barry, crowded as many people aboard as possible, while houses all over town were burning and men and animals collapsed in the street from the heat. The trains were now the only possible avenue of escape. Finally, Best released the air brakes and eased out of the station. Barry followed close behind.

Driven by high winds, the forest fire raced toward the trains with incredible speed, but the engineers could do little to outrun it. They had to crawl along at a dead-slow pace because they could not be certain of the fire-tortured rails in front of them. In places the heat was so intense that the rails began to buckle and twist. Inside the coaches and boxcars, people raved or prayed or sat silent, their white faces caked with soot and streaked with perspiration.

Smoke eclipsed the sun, and the headlamps on the engines glowed feebly in the gloom. Best and Barry could see little or nothing of what lay ahead of them, but they knew this route. Little by little the engineers inched over the twisted track. When they came to a bridge, Best would stop until he could convince himself that the burning bridge would support the train. There were nineteen bridges to cross on the fourteen miles of track north of Hinckley and all nineteen were burning when the Hinckley trains crossed them. Eventually, all would collapse.

When the trains reached the town of Sandstone—so far untouched by the flames—the engineers paused long enough to urge the townspeople on board. Most folks felt they were safe enough in Sandstone, but a few climbed on and the trains continued their run for safety. The smoke grew so thick that Barry lost sight of Best up ahead. He posted two brakemen on the sides of the tender as watchmen. Barry's train slowed when it came to the Kettle River just beyond Sandstone. Here the entire bridge was aflame and it seemed the train and it passengers were hopelessly trapped with the fire already rushing down on them.

"For God's sake!" the brakeman yelled to Barry. "Best made it. Go on! Cross it! The entire bridge will be down in another five minutes."

Barry sucked in his breath, opened the throttle, and raced across the bridge. Sure enough, five minutes after the second train crossed, the trestle timbers began to give way and fall. Then the entire bridge buckled and fell into the river. Behind them, the fire closed in on Sandstone only an hour after the trains had passed through, quickly reducing the town to cinders.

Best and Barry both reached safety along with their crowded trains of refugees, but while they were steaming away from the fire another train was speeding directly into the flames.

When the Southbound Limited left Duluth that September afternoon, its engineer Jim Root and fireman Jack McGowan had no idea of the danger that lay ahead. The crew got worried when smoke began to obscure their view of the tracks. Then, only an hour into their run,

Root and McGowan threw on the brakes. They had never seen anything like this—more than 150 half-crazed, smoke-blackened people had crowded onto the tracks to wait for the Limited. There was no time for these people to tell their story. They scrambled aboard, and the Limited took off.

Soon the fire began to close in around the train. Desperately shoveling coal, McGowan built up all the steam he could in the locomotive, but it soon became apparent that the train could not outrun the flames. Still engineer Root kept pushing the engine for all the speed it would give him. He knew that four miles ahead lay marshy Skunk Lake. If he could make it, his passengers would be safe. Although smoke had obscured his view and the tracks had begun to crumple, he kept the throttle wide open.

In the bucking, twisting coaches, passengers went mad in the heat. One man hurled himself through a window into the flames. Others tried to follow until their saner companions held them back. Things were far worse for the engineer and fireman up in the cab. Root's hands blistered on the throttle and his clothes caught fire. McGowan jumped into the manhole of the water tank to douse his clothes, then dumped buckets of water on the engineer to extinguish *his* clothes. Twice Root fainted, falling from his seat, and twice his faithful fireman revived him. Finally Root threw on the air brakes and the Limited hissed to a stop. They had reached Skunk Lake. An entire trainload of people poured out of their smoldering coaches and dove into the water—safe now from the inferno.

Gauges must have gone wild as firemen stoked for all the speed they could get to outrun the Hinckley fire. ROBERT KIRCHHERR.

I t has been said that great public calamities produce heroes. If that is so, then it is probably also true that small private calamities produce hobos.

What—or who—exactly is a hobo? The definition has never been entirely clear. But most would agree that hobos are people who travel a lot by train, rarely on a passenger line and more rarely still with the benefit of a ticket. Hobos are sometimes confused with other varieties of vagabond such as tramps or bums, but self-respecting hobos would never confuse *themselves* with such people. According to Ben Reitman, who

'Boes Boomers, Bindle Stiffs

Typical of late nineteenth-century engines is this 1880 model belonging to the Black Hills Central Railroad in North Dakota. Doubtless many a hobo rode the rails behind an engine like this. BRUCE ROBERTS.

Living up to its watery name,
a Lake Superior & Mississippi
diesel makes a twelve-mile run
through beautiful Minnesota scenery.
COURTESY LAKE SUPERIOR & MISSISSIPPI
RAILROAD, DULUTH, MINNESOTA.

did some wandering himself, a hobo works and wanders, a tramp dreams and wanders, and a bum drinks and wanders.

No one has ever been sure how many people belonged to the American hobo subculture, but by the turn of the century, there were surely hundreds of thousands of 'boes, boomers, and bindle stiffs wandering about the country. In times of depression, as many as a million men and women were likely riding the rails without tickets, and in most cases with no place to call home. In 1932, the Southern Pacific reported it ejected nearly 700,000 vagrants from its boxcars. Mattoon, Illinois, where the nation's most heavily traveled east–west and north–south mainlines cross, was a hobo capital, a meeting place for people on the move.

Hobos developed a set of signals to relay useful information. Sometimes they marked a house or a even a town as a good place to stop or to avoid. The Green Mountain Flyer in Vermont still crosses some old wooden covered bridges in Bartonsville which were used as a communication network for the hobos who passed through. Notes have been found behind some of the original beams telling fellow travelers where they could get a free meal or a safe place to sleep.

For hobos, accommodations on trains were never first class, but those who knew how could always catch a free ride. They would hide in boxcars or ride the deck (the roof of a boxcar where falling asleep could have fatal consequences), swing aboard the blind (the space between the first baggage car and the locomotive), or ride the rods beneath the freight cars. Wherever they rode, it was dangerous. William Davis, an Englishman bumming around America in the early 1900s told of trying to hop aboard a freight. "My foot came short of the step, I fell, and, still clinging to the handle-bar, was dragged several yards before I relinquished my hold. And there I lay for several minutes, feeling a little shaken, whilst the train passed swiftly into the darkness." At length Davis attempted to stand—only to discover that his foot had been severed at the ankle.

Most rail lines did their best to keep hobos off their trains, not so much on principle as because the stowaways did millions of dollars worth of damage. They lit fires in boxcars to keep warm and tore open and ruined freight searching for small valuables they could carry in their bindles. So the railroads hired bulls—private police—to guard their freight. "The best way to keep tramps off trains or other railroad property is to beat up any unauthorized person you might find in the yards," said one railroad official. "On the trains I might talk a while with tramps riding the boxcars, and then force them to jump, or push them off."

Occasionally, hobos might figure out a way to flag or slow down a train to buy enough time to get aboard. One long-time engineer recalled, "Just as we passed the station, the glare of the headlight picked up what looked to me like a railroad tie across the rails ahead. I slowed down, then came to a full stop and hollered to my fireman to get down and take the tie off the track. That wasn't a tie. It was an inch-board the length of a tie and placed on edge across the rails to look like a tie. When we got to Pennington, I noticed two hobos who were riding on the blind. The fireman was going to put them off, but I told him to let them ride. Any two 'boes as smart as they were, I said, were entitled to ride blind the whole division, if they wanted to."

It wasn't the accidents or the bulls that put an end to hoboing, but the automobile. Although a few tramps still ride the rods, blinds, and boxcars, most wanderers these days use their thumbs to hitch a ride in the comfort of a car.

Wintry weather doesn't stop engines or passengers on the Algoma Central in Ontario. COURTESY ALGOMA CENTRAL RAILROAD.

This line offers a relaxed, early-century feeling. Trains depart from the resort town of French Lick and the old Manon Railroad Station, built about 1910. Plunging into the Hoosier National Forest, passengers are treated to lovely views of rolling wooded hills. This is limestone country, and several deep rock cuts provide amateur geologists with a look at what lies below ground. The passenger cars are old-fashioned but comfortable, and a diesel engine pulls them through the 2,200-foot Burton Tunnel to Cuzco, Indiana, located on picturesque Patoka Lake.

Left: It sometimes takes years to restore an old steam engine to its former glory. BRUCE ROBERTS PHOTO. Right: With an artist's touch, new numbers are hand-painted on a shiny restored car. CHARLIE MAPLE PHOTO; COURTESY TEXAS STATE RAILROAD, RUSK, TEXAS.

FRENCH LICK, WEST BADEN & SOUTHERN RAILWAY

WHERE TO BOARD:
Old Monon RR passenger station in French Lick, on State Route 56, southwestern Indiana.

FOR TICKET INFORMATION:
French Lick Scenic Railway, P.O. Box 150, French Lick, IN 47432. Telephone 812-936-2405.

FARES IN 1992:
Adults $8; Children (3–11) $4. Children under 3 ride free.

LENGTH OF TRIP:
20 miles, 1 3/4 hours round trip.

DATES OF OPERATION:
Weekends April through November.

SCHEDULE:
Train leaves at 10:00 a.m., 1:00 p.m. & 4:00 p.m.

SPECIAL EVENTS:
Wild West Holdups (on regular runs)—April 25–26, May 23–25, July 4–5, Sept. 5–7, & Oct. 24–25.

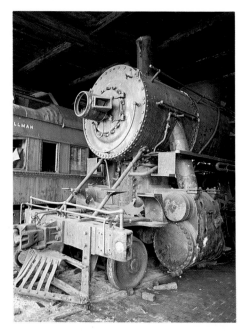

KALAMAZOO, LAKE SHORE & CHICAGO RAILWAY

WHERE TO BOARD:
Fifteen miles west of Kalamazoo in southwestern Michigan. Take exit 60 off I-94; travel north 1/2 mile.

FOR TICKET INFORMATION:
Kalamazoo, Lake Shore & Chicago Railway, Box 178, Paw Paw, MI 49079. Telephone 616-657-5963; dinner train, first class, or Santa reservations: 616-657-7037.

FARES IN 1991:

	Adults	Seniors (65+)	Children (2-11)
Round Trip Excursion	$8	$7	$4
First Class reserved seat (Snack & beverage included)	14	13	7
Caboose seat	10	10	6

Children under 2 ride free. Group rates available.
Luxury Dinner Train—Lunch $39; Dinner $59.

LENGTH OF TRIP:
16 miles, 1 1/2 hour round trip.

DATES OF OPERATION:
Year-round.

SCHEDULE:

Mid-April through June	Sat. & Sun. only—1:00 p.m.
July & August	Wed.–Fri.—1:00 p.m. Sat. & Sun.—1:00 & 3:30 p.m.
September	Mon.–Fri. of first week and Sat. & Sun.— 1:00 p.m. & 3:30 p.m.
October	Weekdays—1:00 p.m. Weekends—1:00, 3:30 & 5:30 p.m.

Write for weekend schedules for November through March.

SPECIAL EVENTS:
Santa Claus Train, Winter Scenic Trains, Dinner Train, Murder Mysteries, and Musical Entertainment.

■ When its 1,500-horsepower engine kicks in, the big General Motors diesel could pull much of the town of Paw Paw over the tracks. However, its load is usually much lighter—a pair of vintage Pullmans and a caboose bound for Michigan's vineyard country. The KLS&C hauls both freight and passengers and offers special dinner trains featuring elegant multi-course meals.

In 1894 a forest fire ran wild through this part of Minnesota consuming several entire towns. Many of those who survived the disaster owe their lives to a last minute escape made possible by a pair of LS&M trains and their heroic crews. Today's passengers won't likely see any forest fires but they will enjoy some delightful views. The twelve-mile trip to New Duluth follows the St. Louis River and crosses Mud Lake on a long trestle. Passengers should plan to visit the Lake Superior Museum of Transportation housed in the castle-like Duluth Union Depot. The museum features several historic engines, including a giant 2-8-8-4 steam locomotive and an abundance of rolling stock and old-time railroad equipment.

LAKE SUPERIOR & MISSISSIPPI RAILROAD

WHERE TO BOARD:
Western Waterfront Trail across from the Lake Superior Zoological Gardens on Grand Ave., Route 23.

From Minneapolis on I-35, exit on Cody St.; turn right at first stop light and right again at next stop light. Follow Hwy. 23 to Zoo.

From east on I-35, exit on Grand Ave., follow Hwy. 23 to Western Waterfront Trail.

FOR TICKET INFORMATION:
LS&M, 506 West Michigan St., Duluth, MN 55802. Telephone 218-624-7549.

FARES IN 1991:
Adults $5; Seniors $4; Children (12 & under) $4.
Charters available.

LENGTH OF TRIP:
12 miles, 1½ hour round trip.

DATES OF OPERATION:
July & August.

SCHEDULE:
Saturdays & Sundays, 11:00 a.m. & 2:00 p.m.

NORTH SHORE SCENIC RAILROAD

WHERE TO BOARD:
506 West Michigan Street in Duluth.

FOR TICKET INFORMATION:
North Shore Scenic Railroad, 506 West Michigan St., Duluth, MN 55802. Telephone 218-722-1273.

FARES IN 1991:

	Adults	Seniors (60+)	Children (3–12)
Duluth to Two Harbors	$15	$14	$7.50
Duluth to Lester River	$8	$7	$4
Two Harbors to Palmer	$8	$7	$4
Sunset Excursion	$11	$10	$5.50

Children under 3 ride free.

LENGTH OF TRIP:
Duluth to Two Harbors: 1 1/2 hours each way with 2 3/4 hours layover.
Duluth to Lester River: 1 hour round trip.
Two Harbors to Palmer: 1 1/2 hours round trip.
Sunset Excursion: 2 hours round trip.

DATES OF OPERATION:
Mid-April through mid-October.

SCHEDULE:
DULUTH TO TWO HARBORS

LV Duluth	AR T.H.	LV T.H.	AR Duluth

Mid-April through May, Sat. & Sun.

LV Duluth	AR T.H.	LV T.H.	AR Duluth
11:30 a.m.	1:00 p.m.	2:30 p.m.	4:00 p.m.

June to Sept. 1, Daily except Monday

11:30 a.m.	1:00 p.m.	3:45 p.m.	5:00 p.m.

Sept. 3–mid-Oct., Thu.–Sun.

11:30 a.m.	1:00 p.m.	3:45 p.m.	5:00 p.m.

DULUTH TO LESTER RIVER round trip—June to Sept. 1, daily except Tuesday. LV Duluth 10:00 a.m., noon, 2:00 & 4:00 p.m.

TWO HARBORS TO PALMER round trip
June to Sept. 1, Tue.-Sun.—LV Two Harbors 1:30 p.m.
Mid-Sept. to Mid-Oct., Thu.-Sun.—LV Two Harbors 1:30 p.m.

SUNSET EXCURSION daily starting June 26—LV Duluth 6:00 p.m.

■ Following the north shore of Lake Superior on the route of the old Duluth, Missabe & Iron Range Railroad, the NSSR line treats passengers to views of woods and water. Along the way they'll also see much of the Duluth waterfront, ore docks, an aerial lift bridge, the taconite rail yard, and the Knife River.

An enthusiastic youngster prepares for the ride of his life. BRUCE ROBERTS.

The eighteen-mile excursion trip over a standard-gauge line completed in 1871 carries passengers to a place called Peculiar. A 1,200-horsepower Baldwin diesel does the pulling. The line is operated by the Smoky Hill Railroad Museum in Belton which features more than sixty pieces of rolling stock including historic steam and diesel locomotives, venerable passenger and freight cars, and plenty of railroad equipment. Among the locomotives on display is an 8,500-horsepower gas turbine engine built by General Electric in 1960.

Smoky Hill Railway

WHERE TO BOARD:
502 Walnut in downtown Belton—30 minutes south of Kansas City on Highway 71.

FOR TICKET INFORMATION:
Smoky Hill Railway Museum, P.O. Box 224, Grandview, MO 64030. Telephone 816-331-0630.

FARES IN 1991:
Adults $4; Juniors (under 18) $2.50

LENGTH OF TRIP:
18 miles, 1½ hour round trip.

DATES OF OPERATION:
Late May to early September.

SCHEDULE:
Thursday–Monday—please call or write for schedule.

SPECIAL EVENTS:
Dining Car Exposition, Railroad Art Festival.

St. Louis, Iron Mountain & Southern Railway

WHERE TO BOARD:
Depot in Jackson—intersection of highways 61, 25, 72 & 34.

FOR TICKET INFORMATION:
St. Louis, Iron Mountain & Southern Railway, P.O. Box 244, Jackson, MO 63755. Telephone 314-243-1688.

FARES IN 1991:
Adults $8; Children (3–12 yrs. old) $4; age 2 & under free.
Dinner Train $22. Reservations required.
Charters and group rates available.

LENGTH OF TRIP:
Jackson to Gordonville—10 miles, 1¼ hours round trip; Jackson to Dutchtown dinner trip—18 miles, 2 hours round trip.

DATES OF OPERATION:
April through October with steam. Winter specials with diesel.

SCHEDULE:
Jackson to Gordonville
Saturdays—11:00 a.m. & 2:00 p.m.
Sundays—1:00 p.m. & 3:00 p.m.
Wednesdays (June–Aug.)—1:00 p.m.

Dinner Train—Jackson to Dutchtown
Saturdays—6:00 p.m.

SPECIAL EVENTS:
Murder Mystery, Darren's Magic Express, Easter, Train Robbery, Bonnie & Clyde, Mother's Day, Father's Day, Indian Weekend, Hobo Party, Haunted Train, Senior's Day, Fall Foliage Breakfast, Santa's Express, New Year's Eve.

■ Steam provides the power and history provides the drama on this southeastern Missouri line. During the ride, a reenactment of the Civil War battle at Pilot's Knob reminds passengers of the important role this railway played in that brother-against-brother conflict. A staged James-gang robbery at Gads Hill adds another touch of fun and frontier spirit to the experience. The railroad itself has been running since 1858. Its central location insured success as a passenger and freight carrier and made it a key participant in the Civil War.

Engine No. 5 thunders over a trestle on the St. Louis, Iron Mountain & Southern scenic run.
PHOTO BY JIM HURTLE; COURTESY ST. LOUIS, IRON MOUNTAIN & SOUTHERN RAILROAD.

This train repeatedly crosses paths with history—for instance the 1840s Mormon Trail, an historic Indian trail, and the route of Major Stephen Long's 1820s western military expedition. There is plenty of scenery, too, as a diesel pulls 1940s-vintage coaches through the beautiful Elkhorn River valley on a portion of the former Chicago & Northwestern mainline to the Black Hills. The FEVR serves dinners with 1940s-style elegance —complete with Big Band music, shaded lamps, folded napkins, red plush draperies, silver, and crystal.

FREMONT & ELKHORN VALLEY RAILROAD

WHERE TO BOARD:
FEVR Depot at 1835 North Somers Ave. in Fremont off Highway 30. From Lincoln, I-80 to Fremont, 45 mi.; Omaha to Fremont, 27 mi.

FOR TICKET INFORMATION:
FEVR, 1835 N. Somers Ave., Fremont, NE 68025. Telephone 402-727-0615; 800-942-RAIL (800-942-7245).

FARES IN 1991:

	Adults	Children (12 & under)
Excursion:	$11	$6
Air-conditioned cars if available	$16	$8
To Nickerson	$6	$4

Dinner Train:	
Saturday Luncheon	$30.50
Fri. & Sat. Dinners	$37.50
Sunday Dinner	$34.50

Prices include meals and rail fare; taxes & gratuities not included. Children's rates are available.

LENGTH OF TRIP: 30 miles, 3 hour round trip.

DATES OF OPERATION: Year-round.

SCHEDULE:
FREMONT TO HOOPER EXCURSION

Sundays	Apr., Nov., Dec.—LV 1:30 p.m.; RET 4:15–4:30 p.m.
	May–Oct.—LV 2:00 p.m.; RET 4:45–5:00 p.m.
Saturdays	May–Oct.—LV 1:00 p.m.; RET 3:45–4:00 p.m.

Additional Runs in June–August, Mon.–Fri.—2:00 p.m. to Nickerson (16 miles round trip returning approx. 3:15 p.m.)

DINNER TRAIN:	Board	Depart	Return
Friday Dinner	7:00–7:15 p.m.	7:30 p.m.	10:15–10:30 p.m.
Sat. Luncheon	12:30–12:45 p.m.	1:00 p.m.	3:45–4:00 p.m.

2nd & 4th Saturdays, June to October.

Saturday Dinner			
Nov.–Mar.	6:00–6:15 p.m.	6:30 p.m.	9:15–9:30 p.m.
Apr.–Oct.	7:00–7:15 p.m.	7:30 p.m.	10:15–10:30 p.m.
Sunday Dinner	1:00–1:15 p.m.	1:30 p.m.	4:45–5:00 p.m.

SPECIAL EVENTS:
Murder Mystery Runs, holiday runs, gambling car, USO shows.

OHIO CENTRAL RAILROAD

WHERE TO BOARD:
Depot at 111 Factory Street in Sugarcreek. Take I-77 to Dover Exit, turn west on Ohio Rte. 39, drive 15 minutes to Sugarcreek. Turn left at the first stoplight onto Factory Street. Follow Factory Street to downtown—the station and ticket office are on the left.

FOR TICKET INFORMATION:
Ohio Central Railroad, P.O. Box 427, Sugarcreek, OH 44681. Telephone 216-852-4676.

FARES IN 1992:
Adults (13 and older) $6; Children (3–12) $4. Children under 3 ride free. Group rates available.

LENGTH OF TRIP:
12 miles, 1-hour round trip.

DATES OF OPERATION:
May 1 through last Saturday of October.

SCHEDULE:
May 1 through mid-June
Mon.–Sat.—11:00 a.m., 1:00 & 3:00 p.m.

Mid-June through Labor Day
Mon.–Sat.—11:00 a.m., 12:30, 2:00 & 3:30 p.m.

First Tue. after Labor Day through last Sat. of October.
Mon.–Sat.—11:00 a.m.,. 1:00 & 3:00 p.m.

SPECIAL EVENTS:
Annual Ohio Swiss Festival Special (Fourth weekend after Labor Day).

A branch of the former Wheeling & Lake Erie Railroad, this line was built in 1882. Originally it was known as the Connotton Valley Railroad and then as the Cleveland, Canton & Southern, which provided rail service between Cleveland and Zanesville. The Sugar Creek depot dates back to 1915 when its predecessor was destroyed in a fire. An Amish community, Sugar Creek grew up around the depot. The train, pulled by a big 1912 Montreal 4-6-0, offers an excellent view of the verdant Amish farmlands.

Amish lads wave a greeting as the vintage Ohio Central rumbles through the farmland. DOYLE YODER PHOTOGRAPHY. BERLIN, OHIO; COURTESY OHIO CENTRAL RAILROAD.

■ The I&OSR is a working common-carrier freight and passenger line operating in southwestern Ohio. Originally part of the old Cincinnati, Lebanon & Northern narrow-gauge railroad, for many years it served as a branch of the Pennsylvania Railroad. Diesel provides the pulling power on today's sixteen-mile scenic excursions. Coaches are electric commuter cars built about 1930.

INDIANA & OHIO SCENIC RAILWAY

WHERE TO BOARD:
Mason Depot on Forest and Western avenues in Mason on US 42 north of Cincinnati.

FOR TICKET INFORMATION:
Indiana & Ohio Scenic Railway, P.O. Box 8150, West Chester, OH 45069. Telephone 513-777-5777; group reservations (20 or more) 513-398-8584.

FARES IN 1991:
Adults $8; Children (12 & under) $4. Season Passes: Adults $20; Children $10. Group rates available.

LENGTH OF TRIP:
16 miles, 2 hours round trip.

DATES OF OPERATION:
Saturdays, Sundays & holidays from early May to late November, plus special Christmas trips.

SCHEDULE:
Depart Mason noon & 2:30 p.m.
Depart Lebanon 1:00 p.m. & 3:00 p.m.*
*One way to Mason only.

SPECIAL EVENTS:
Mother's Day, Father's Day, Halloween, Family Day, Ice Cream Social, Golden Lamb Luncheon Tours, Christmas in Lebanon.

ALGOMA CENTRAL RAILWAY

WHERE TO BOARD:
Depot at 129 Bay Street in Sault Ste. Marie.

FOR TICKET INFORMATION:
Passenger Sales, Algoma Central Railway, 129 Bay St., Sault Ste. Marie, 20, Ontario P6A 1W7, Canada. Telephone 705-946-7300.

FARES IN 1992:
Agawa Canyon Tour—Adults $42.75; Children & high school students (June, July, & Aug.) $16.25; Children & high school students (Sept. & Oct.) $21.40; Children under 5 years $7.55; Babes in arms free. Special fare June 8–30 for seniors (60+) $30.10.

Sault Ste. Marie to Hearst—Adults $99; Children/Students $49.50; under 5 free.
Prices quoted in Canadian funds. Fares include all applicable taxes.

LENGTH OF TRIP:
Agawa Canyon Tour: 228 miles, 9-hour round trip. Sault Ste. Marie to Hearst: 300 miles, two-day round trip including overnight stay in Hearst.

DATES OF OPERATION:
Agawa Canyon Tour: daily early June to mid-October. Through train to Hearst operates year-round. Snow Train: weekends late December to mid-March.

SCHEDULE:
AGAWA CANYON TOUR:

LV Sault Ste. Marie	8:00 a.m.
ARR Agawa Canyon	11:30 a.m.
LV Agawa Canyon	1:30 p.m.
ARR Sault Ste. Marie	5:00 p.m.

HEARST:
Northbound, Fri., Sat., & Sun.

LV Sault Ste. Marie	9:00 a.m.
ARR Hearst	6:20 p.m.

Southbound, Sat., Sun., & Mon.

LV Hearst	8:00 a.m.
ARR Sault Ste. Marie	5:00 p.m.

■ On a day-long round trip to Agawa Canyon, the handsome gray and maroon diesel-electric locomotive heads north out of Sault Ste. Marie, past ageless granite rock formations of the Canadian shield, through mixed forests of maple, birch, and pine, and along pristine rivers feeding into Lake Superior. From picture windows, passengers can see rocky outcrops and deep mountain gorges where Ojibway Indians, fur traders, lumberjacks, and prospectors once made their home. The train coasts down five hundred feet through a narrow cut in the mountains to the floor of the Agawa Canyon. Here passengers are allowed plenty of time to enjoy a picnic and explore the canyon's waterfalls, hiking trails, and park.

Since the Nicolet operates as a short-line common carrier, passengers can enjoy watching freight operations, mostly involving forest products. Located in northeastern Wisconsin, the line runs through the Nicolet National Forest. This is lumberjack country, and scenery includes densely forested landscape and glistening lakes as well as beaver dams, lodges, and ponds.

SHELBY BROWN
5

They've got a ticket to ride, and they'll love it—anywhere there's a working railroad. COURTESY ST. LOUIS, IRON MOUNTAIN & SOUTHERN RAILROAD.

NICOLET SCENIC RAIL

WHERE TO BOARD:
Laona, northeastern Wisconsin, US Highway 8 and WI Highway 32.

FOR TICKET INFORMATION:
Nicolet Scenic Rail, P.O. Box 310, Laona, WI 54541. Telephone 800-752-1465, 715-674-6309.

FARES IN 1991:
Laona to Wabeno, round trip: Adults $10.50; Seniors $9; Students (6–15) $7.

Laona to Tipler, round trip, including buffet: Adults $32; Seniors $29; Students $24.

Charters available.

LENGTH OF TRIP:
Laona to Wabeno, 18-mile 2$^{1}/_{4}$ hour round trip. Laona to Tipler, 60-mile, 5-hour round trip including dinner break at Long Lake.

DATES OF OPERATION:
Thursday–Saturday, late June to early October.

SCHEDULE:
LAONA TO WABENO

Thurs.	LV Laona	AR Wabeno	LV Wabeno	AR Laona
	10:30 a.m.	11:15 a.m.	Noon	12:45 p.m.
	1:45 p.m.	2:30 p.m.	3:15 p.m.	4:00 p.m.
Sat. & Sun.	11:00 a.m.	11:45 a.m.	12:45 p.m.	1:30 p.m.

LAONA TO TIPLER

Sat. & Sun.	LV Laona	AR Long Lake	LV Long Lake	AR Laona
	4:30 p.m.	5:45 p.m.	7:10 p.m.	9:30 p.m.

SPECIAL EVENTS:
Colorama Trains in Sept. & Oct. Snow Trains in winter.

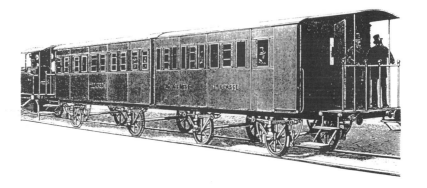

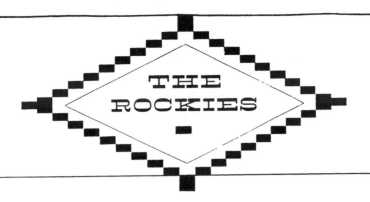

WARS

In the Rocky Mountains railroads are as much a part of the pioneer story as ranchers, outlaws, and gold strikes. If covered wagons and mule trains helped to settle this rugged western region, so did steam locomotives. Abraham Lincoln and Horace Greeley both predicted it would be one hundred years before the West was settled, but the railroads cut that time in half.

Fighting Through the Passes

The ringing blows that drove home the golden spike in Promontory, Utah, in 1869 were like a conductor's call of "All aboard!" After that, anybody who wanted a piece of the West had better get on the train. The big transcontinental lines—the Northern Pacific, the Kansas Pacific, the Atchison, Topeka & the Santa Fe, the Denver & Rio Grande, the Burlington, and the Great Northern—treated the West as a business. In fact, the western land that folks wanted to settle was often part of their business since the federal goverment had deeded them huge tracts to help finance their ventures.

Generally speaking, people take money seriously, but the bearded tycoons who pushed their transcontinental lines through the Rockies raised greed to new heights—literally. These great railroads might never have been built save for some extraordinary feats of engineering and the back-breaking labor of underpaid immigrant construction crews, but the

Where the railroad builders couldn't go around the mountains, they went *through* them, with hundreds of just-big-enough tunnels. DUNCAN RICHARDS.

true driving force behind them was the ambition of their owners. The western railroad tycoons were men of great vision, but they were also capable of considerable chicanery, and they never let their scruples stand in the way of another section of track. It mattered little to them where the tracks were laid so long as they stretched on toward the Pacific. The gentlemen whose sober-faced portraits still grace the boardrooms of some of these lines were often no gentlemen. Had they been in another profession, their faces might just as easily have appeared on wanted posters. Never flinching, they hired thugs and even notorious gunslingers to carve out rights of way with bullets. In the middle of the night they laid track over the land of ranchers who had refused to sell. And when people turned to the law for help, the "gentlemen" bribed sheriffs, judges, legislators, territorial governors, and when necessary, U.S. senators. They were railroad warriors battling for possession of the West, carving up the land with the sword of their ruthlessness.

It seemed that even the land itself was caught up in the railroad mania gripping the region. Towns popped up along the tracks, each of them dependent on their railroad and feeding on it like a buffalo on the range grass. The Atchison & Topeka (which later added "Santa Fe" to its name when it decided to push westward) created one legendary cow town after another. There was Newton, dubbed "Shootin' Newton" after the celebrations of cowhands who had delivered steers to the railhead. There was Dodge City, the solitary town on the Kansas prairie: It needed a jail before the steam cars could even deliver lumber for the buildings. So the enterprising citizens of the new town dug a hole in the ground and used that as a lockup for the drunk, the disorderly, and the downright ornery.

One nineteenth century English traveler reported seeing a long, ragged freight grind to a stop beside a collection of shacks straggled out on either side of the tracks in Wyoming. In the train were carloads of lumber, canvas tents, signs, walls, everything a western town might need right down to barber chairs and pool tables. A disreputable looking crowd assembled at the makeshift station to see what all this meant. The conductor cleared things up for them. "Gentlemen," he said, pointing at the train, "here is Julesberg." Lithographs of imagined comforts and splendors—parks, broad streets, hotels, and theaters—were sent back east to draw settlers to towns like Julesberg. When newcomers stepped down from their train coaches, the reality confronting them seldom matched what the pictures suggested, but perhaps that was just as well. Many of them brought saws, hammers, and nails with them, and they had a dream to serve as a blueprint.

Railroads were by their very nature monopolistic. Usually only one line served a given area. When two or more lines slammed into each other at the margins of these territories, sparks flew. In the 1870s, the early days of railroading in the Rockies, the Santa Fe and the Denver & Rio Grande both tried to build through Raton Pass, the narrow gateway leading from the high plains of Colorado to New Mexico. The two railroads resorted to every sort of double dealing in order to be first through the pass. Hoping to grab an advantage, the Santa Fe rushed surveyor Albert Robinson to the pass. At Pueblo, Colorado, Robinson boarded the only train available—operated by the rival Denver & Rio Grande. In the smoker Robinson noticed Rio Grande surveyor J.A. McMurtie. Each man guessed the other's mission.

McMurtie recruited an armed force in El Moro, marched to the base of the pass, and set up camp, confident that he had taken a firm grip on the right of way. Meanwhile Robinson rode hellbent for leather to Trinidad, a town bypassed by the Rio Grande. Promising to lay Santa Fe tracks through Trinidad, Robinson recruited a small but enthusiastic party of local boosters armed with shovels and rifles. When McMurtie's men woke up the next morning, they discovered the Santa Fe crew had slipped past them in the night and taken firm possession of the pass. Tracks followed close on the heels of Robinson's well-armed surveyors, and the first Santa Fe train came through Raton Pass in 1878.

That same year, the fierce rivalry between the two lines moved into another, even more spectacular arena, the Grand Canyon of the Arkansas. At Raton, the two railroads had fought a minor guerilla action, but here in the 3,000-foot-deep gorge of the Arkansas River, their confrontation turned into an all-out shooting war. Doorway to the extraordinar-

On September 17, 1901, the first passengers to arrive by scheduled steam train disembarked at the South Rim of the Grand Canyon. COURTESY NATIONAL PARK SERVICE. Eighty-nine years later, passenger service was reinstated on the scenic route from Williams, Arizona, to the Canyon. COURTESY GRAND CANYON RAILROAD.

ily rich silver mining country around Leadville, the canyon was a prize that neither side could ignore, and both lines were determined to snatch it for themselves. The fast-moving Santa Fe made the first grab at the canyon, secretly dispatching an engineer named Morley to Colorado. However, the Santa Fe plan to lay tracks through the canyon turned out

The towering Rockies made construction of a railroad unlikely here, but creative engineering produced the fascinating Georgetown Loop.
COURTESY GEORGETOWN LOOP RAILROAD.

not to be a secret after all. The Denver & Rio Grande owned all the telegraph lines in Colorado and made a policy of intercepting and reading all telegrams sent by their competitors, particularly the Santa Fe. As a consequence, they were privy to every move Morley made.

Morley had intended to quietly take a D&RG passenger train to Canyon City, a small Colorado town near his goal. Rio Grande officials made sure none of their trains in the area were running and Morley was forced to ride more than sixty miles cross-country on horseback to reach the canyon. Meanwhile, a force of a hundred armed men steamed westward on a special, bent on taking control of the canyon for the Rio Grande. When they arrived, however, the D&RG discovered that the hard-riding Morley had gotten there first and raised a war party of his own. Morley posted riflemen behind strategic boulders to keep watch while other men started work with shovels, picks, and sledges. Not to be deterred, the D&RG army marched around their enemy and blocked Morley's path with a series of forts, all bristling with Winchesters.

When an army of lawyers tried to take the matter out of the hands of the gunmen, the resulting legal snarl became so tangled that even the Colorado supreme court was unable to cut through the knot. The two sides were then left to resolve the matter in the old-fashioned western way—with rifles and pistols. Having the larger army, the Rio Grande quickly isolated their opponents in Canyon City and escalated the fighting by marching on the Santa Fe railyards in Pueblo. Along the way, they captured one Santa Fe depot after another, forcibly evicting the employees. But the Rio Grande war party faced a tougher challenge in Pueblo. There notorious gunman and Dodge City Marshall Bat Masterson waited, holed up in the Santa Fe roundhouse with a gang of tough riflemen. Rather than attempt an armed frontal assault, the Rio Grande force employed a tried-and-true negotiating technique: bribery. They sent the corporate treasurer—an unusually brave fellow—into the roundhouse with a valise stuffed with money. Preferring the rustle of cold cash to the crack of hot lead, Masterson and his minions dispersed.

For several months sporadic fighting continued with sabotage, beatings, kidnappings, and occasional gunplay. But the Rio Grande had outmaneuvered and outshot its rival. Eventually, reaffirming the old legal principle that "possession is nine-tenths of the law," the Colorado supreme court put the stamp of law on the status quo, and it was over.

Incidentally, all the shooting helped some railroad employees improve their marksmanship, a skill which was to prove useful in unlikely situations. For instance, one sharpshooting Santa Fe conductor used his pistol to stop an otherwise certain collision. When his train was stopped by a washout near Cimarron, Kansas, the conductor braved a driving rain and hurried down the tracks with a red lantern to warn a fast-approaching freight. Blinded by the rain, the engineer missed the warning and barreled on toward the stalled train and the washout. A veteran of the recently concluded railroad war, the conductor still kept a Colt .45 on his hip. So he drew the pistol and let fly, shooting out an air hose between the last two passenger cars and stopping the train.

Railroad Fever in Durango

uring the 1870s and 1880s, no corner of the West, however remote, was spared from the plague of railroad fever gripping the region. If a town could not attract the services of a line, its people drifted off to other towns that did have a railroad. Sometimes the whole town was moved, its hardware stores, barber shops, brothels, and town offices torn down or abandoned and rebuilt beside a handy set of tracks.

Often, new towns were built in anticipation of a railroad. Even the suggestion that a railroad might be coming through could cause people to start throwing up buildings. For instance, the town of Durango, Colorado, owes its existence to a newspaper story about a proposed Denver & Rio Grande line through the Animas River Valley to the rich mines at Silverton. The editor of the Animas City *Southwest* noted that the tracks were to run through the "new town of Durango. Where the . . . town . . . is to be, or not to be, God and the D&RG Railroad only know. If they are in cahoots, we ask for special dispensation." Soon the editor was forced to stop poking fun at Durango, as most residents of his own Animas City had packed up and moved there. Within a few months the editor himself had relocated to the new railroad town, carrying his

The depot at Durango looks much as it did in 1881.
COURTESY DURANGO & SILVERTON NARROW-GAUGE RAILROAD, DURANGO, COLORADO.

press along with him. In the spring of 1881, it was reported that Durango had one thousand people, fifty-nine places to buy liquor, and one church. But the railroad had still not arrived.

Several decades earlier, New England poet Emily Dickinson had written about the railroad's coming to her own picturesque town of Amherst, "The great railroad decision has been made and there is great rejoicing throughout the town. . . . Everybody is wide awake, everybody is stirring, and the streets are full of people walking cheerily. Nobody believes it yet, it seems like a fairy tale, the most miraculous event in the lives of all of us."

The approach of the Denver & Rio Grande was no less miraculous for the people of Durango. As the last spikes were driven into the 200 miles of narrow-gauge track that would link Alamosa to Durango, townspeople laid plans for the biggest celebration anyone had ever seen in those parts. The party was scheduled for August 1881 to coincide with the arrival of the first official D&RG train.

The event would feature the town's most prized possession (except for its new railroad depot)—a piano. Much to the relief of the D&RG Welcoming Committee, the piano reached Durango ahead of the tracks. Brought from the East to the rail terminus at Bear Creek, it made the rest of the journey over the mountains to Durango by wagon and mule. Once in town, the piano quickly became the focal point for Durango society. Most residents of this remote mountain area had never *seen* a piano, let alone heard one. It was the sort of instrument a person might expect to enjoy in far-off Denver but not in Durango. So the piano was a source of great civic pride for the citizenry and shed a certain metropolitan luster on the community. In August Durango's piano was lovingly placed at the San Juan and New York Smelter, the only building in town large enough to hold the 500 people expected for the gala railroad ball.

To accompany the piano, the town organized its own Durango Band, and brought in a rather notorious ensemble of musicians from the Terrible Mine at Clear Creek. This latter group, known widely and unflatteringly as the Terrible Silver Cornet Band, assaulted ears on a variety of local social occasions. Feeling between the rival bands ran high until it was decided that the musicians' honors should be shared. The Durango Band would play "Hail to the Chief" for the governor while the

Almost higher than the treetops, a steel trestle carries the Cumbres & Toltec locomotive and her cars safely over a gorge. COURTESY CUMBRES & TOLTEC SCENIC RAILROAD.

"Steel, smoke and steam" cross a high trestle above a river, typical of railroad lines in the Rocky Mountain states. COURTESY DURANGO & SILVERTON NARROW-GAUGE RAILROAD, DURANGO, COLORADO.

Terrible Band would lead the grand march at the ball with "The World Turned Upside Down."

When the big day came, the celebration got off to slow start. The D&RG special bringing the governor and other dignitaries from Denver was slowed to a crawl by washouts in the mountains. Passengers found it prudent to walk beside the coaches while the engineer eased the empty cars over groaning tracks that threatened to give way at any second. Meanwhile, the Terrible Silver Cornet Band killed time and tuned instruments at the Nose Paint Saloon, and miners down from Silverton for the occasion visited one of Durango's three rival barber shops, strolled past the town's Hanging Tree, or stopped in at some of the town's fifty-nine drinking establishments. More genteel visitors used the time to visit the baby daughter of John and Ella Pierson, the first child born in Durango and the object of solicitude for miles around.

Finally, at six o'clock that evening, a train whistle and the bark of Colt .45s announced the arrival of the governor's special. Miners and musicians poured out of the saloons. In the excitement of the moment, the rival bands forgot their truce, one striking up the "Anvil Chorus" and the other the National Anthem. The miners added to the music with staccato pistol shots. During the delirious festivities that followed, the citizens of Durango and their visitors ate five whole oxen, a dozen sheep, and two wagonloads of bread. They also drank four barrels of coffee and an unreported volume of liquor. Fortunately, no one was injured during the feasting, although one man got his leg stuck in a barrel of whiskey.

Then it was off to the Smelter for the railroad ball. Here the star of the show was the much-admired Durango piano, although some local ladies tried to take center stage by showing off the latest satin and silk

Engine No. 40 waits patiently for her passengers before the picturesque East Ely depot.
COURTESY NEVADA NORTHERN RAILWAY.

brocade fashions ordered from the *Godey's Ladies Book*. Apparently, firearms were not checked at the door. During one of the waltzes, a slightly drunken cowpoke shot out several of the Smelter's coal oil lamps before he was dragged out and thrown in jail.

Like other frontier railroad towns, Durango was no stranger to gunplay. In fact, it attracted far more than its share of pistol-packing bad men, many of whom came to justice on the Hanging Tree. The town set a record of sorts for swift justice when a gunman descended from a Rio Grande Pullman, visited the Nose Paint Saloon, shot up a bank, and was hanged from the Tree, all within three hours.

Durango is far less violent today, although it is still lively and retains much of its frontier spirit. While the town is no longer known as a hangout for gunslingers, it is notorious for the herds of elk that wander aimlessly into town and stop traffic. The elk usually don't hurt anybody, but they can do serious damage to the car of any unwary motorist who slams into one. During warm weather months, trains still make the run to Silverton. Pulled by narrow-gauge steam locomotives, they provide passengers with one of the wildest and most authentic scenic railroad experiences in America.

"WANTED: Young women, 18–30 years of age, of good character, attractive and intelligent, as waitresses in the Harvey Eating Houses on the Santa Fe Railroad in the West. Good wages with room and meals furnished. Experience not necessary. Write Fred Harvey, Union Depot, Kansas City, Mo."

Mr. Harvey's Girls

This advertisement placed in the *Toledo Blade* and other eastern newspapers must have excited many of the young women who read it. When it first appeared, during the late 1800s, opportunities for women were limited mostly to school teaching or matrimony. In fact, thousands of women answered this and similar ads. Their adventure would begin with a train trip to Missouri for training, then they would set out for the western mountains to work as Harvey Girls.

On a handshake, Fred Harvey had worked out a deal with the Santa Fe Railroad. Santa Fe trains would carry food and supplies for

With the mountains at their back, two vintage engines are on the move.
COURTESY GEORGETOWN LOOP RAILROAD, GEORGETOWN, COLORADO.

Like the steam engines that worked these tracks over a hundred years ago, this diesel today hauls passengers to the top of the continent in the Colorado mountains near Leadville.
PHOTO BY FRANK W. OSTERWALD; COURTESY LEADVILLE, COLORADO & SOUTHERN RAILROAD.

Harvey's chain of restaurants, and his Harvey Houses would feed the railroad's passengers and crew the best food in the West. Serving those meals would be the Harvey Girls, each of them dressed in black shoes and stockings, a black dress with an Elsie collar, a black bow, a white apron, and perhaps a modest hair ribbon.

A Harvey Girl had to be "morally decent," or at least very careful. There was a ten o'clock curfew strictly enforced by fierce dormitory matrons. Despite the matrons and a signed pledge to work for at least a year without marrying, it is estimated that 5,000 Harvey Girls married Santa Fe employees and brought hundreds of babies christened Fred or Harvey or both into the world. In the wild West where socializing was mostly limited to saloons and brothels, Harvey Houses became known as places to meet "nice girls."

At the suggestion of one of his "girls," Harvey built his restaurants in a distinctive Spanish style. The buildings housed a kitchen, dining room, lunch counter, parlor, storerooms, and dormitory all under one roof. The kitchen fixed meals at regular hours, but employees turned out at 2:00 AM if necessary to feed Santa Fe passengers delayed by avalanches, landslides, or Indians. If a train ran late, the conductor would hop off the and wire ahead to the next Harvey House. When the train arrived, a brass gong sounded, and the staff stood at attention while dozens of famished travelers descended on the tables set with starched white linen, gleaming silver, and sparkling glassware. No matter how late the hour, the friendly young waitresses were neatly dressed and courteous.

Management made frequent unannounced inspections to make sure there were no dirty aprons, nicked plates, bent spoons, or frayed napkins. No doubt more than a few well-wishing train conductors wired their Harvey House friends to warn them when management was on the way. Sometimes inspections were made in person by Fred Harvey, a slender, bearded man always dressed in black. When Harvey encountered an excellent waitress—and most of his were quite good—he slipped an especially generous tip beneath his saucer.

Pale purple menu cards in metal holders revealed an astonishing bill of fare. A typical menu listed over thirty items such as "Filet of White-fish; Roast Sirloin of Beef with Boiled Sweet Potatoes, Asparagus, and Sugar Beets; Ragout of Mutton with Green Peas; Apple Pie and Mince Pie with New York Ice Cream." You could have a complete meal for six bits (75¢) in the dining room. At the lunch counter it was pay as you go. Each waitress served two tables set for eight, or up to sixteen people. Steaming platters of meat, pots of coffee or tea, pitchers of water or milk circulated.

> Ample time will be given for all to finish before
> the train leaves. Do not hurry, ladies and gentle-
> men. No one will be left behind.
>
> THE MANAGER

When the last cup of coffee was drunk and the last satisfied diner left to reboard the train, a tired waitress might find a dime or even a quarter under a saucer to add to her $17.50 monthly wage.

Powerful as well as colorful, an Acheson, Topeka & Santa Fe diesel roars out of a mountain tunnel. DUNCAN RICHARDS.

On a busy day a waitress at the lunch counter might attend to the needs of a preacher with a traveling tent revival meeting, an expert from the U.S. Geological Survey, a soberly dressed older woman in an amazing hat whom whisperers claimed was the madame of an itinerent fandango house, half a dozen "hoggers" grimed with soot from the train, a pair of grubstaked partners who left a gold nugget as a tip, a self-taught dentist who used raw whiskey as an anesthetic, a drift of dusty workers from the stamp mill, tourists out to see the real West, someone scouting for a medicine show, several heavily painted ladies whose manners were so correct they were painful, a booking agent for Buffalo Bill's Wild West Show, a lecturer in phrenology, a dignified drunken man who complained there were no raw oysters, a tintype photographer, cattlemen, miners, prospectors, a rainmaker, and assorted town riffraff.

Fred Harvey served the best food in the West, and by the time he died in 1901, he and the Santa Fe owned fifteen hotels, forty-seven restaurants, and thirty dining cars. Theirs was no greasy food flung at harried customers to choke down before the next train, but an honest meal at an honest price well-served by thousands of young women who stayed on to settle in the West.

GRAND CANYON RAILWAY

WHERE TO BOARD:
Grand Canyon Railway Depot—From I-40 in Williams take Exit 163, Grand Canyon Blvd. 1/2 mile south. Thirty miles west of Flagstaff.

FOR TICKET INFORMATION:
Grand Canyon Railway, 518 E. Bill Williams Ave., Williams, AZ 86046. Telephone, reservations only, 1-800-THE TRAIN (1-800-843-8724); group information and rates 1-800-843-8723; other inquiries 602-635-4000.

FARES IN 1992:

		Family Plan*	
	Adults	Children (12 & Under)	Teens (13–19)
Round trip	$54.81	$15.67	$25.40
One way	45.08	12.43	20.54

*Family Plan: For children and teens traveling with adult family members child fare is half the regular child fare and teen fare is half the regular adult fare. Not to be used in conjunction with other discounts or promotions. Subject to availability. Fares include tax and National Park Service entry fee where applicable.

Group rates available. (25 or more)

LENGTH OF TRIP:
64 miles, 2 1/2 hours one way between Williams and South Rim Depot at Grand Canyon.

DATES OF OPERATION:
Fri., Sat., & Sun.—February & November.
Wed. through Sun.—March, April, May & October.
Daily—June through September.
Sat. & Sun.—December, plus daily Dec. 26–31.

SCHEDULE:

LV Williams	9:30 a.m.
AR Grand Canyon	Noon
LV Grand Canyon	4:00 p.m.
AR Williams	6:30 p.m.

SPECIAL EVENTS:
Memorial Day, July Fourth, Thanksgiving weekend, Man Against Machine Bike Race (1st weekend in Oct.).

■ Starting from the Williams Depot and Fray Marcos Hotel, once a bustling Harvey House, the train follows the original sixty-four mile railway route through Arizona to the Grand Canyon. Built in 1901 by the Santa Fe to take passengers to the then little-known Grand Canyon, the railroad replaced a grinding, rib-rattling eight-hour stagecoach ride from Flagstaff. It was abandoned for some years, but was recently restored as a tourist line. A 1910, 2-8-0 steam locomotive brings passengers to the original two-story ponderosa log depot built right on the South Rim of the Canyon.

The "High Line" route is a round trip of about twenty miles that takes passengers to timberline and within sight of Fremont Pass and the Climax Mine. Although today the High Line is diesel operated, it's still the highest railroad in North America and the best place left to gain a firsthand historical perspective on the difficulties and dangers of mountain railroading. Trains roll over the original narrow-gauge rail bed that was constructed in 1883 for shipping silver, lead, and molybdenum eastward out of the mountains. The line still crosses avalanche chutes and winds its way along cliffs with sheer rock walls on one side and steep drop-offs on the other. Wheel flanges still squeal on the tight hairpin turns, just as they did on the original High Line a century ago.

LEADVILLE · COLORADO

LEADVILLE, COLORADO & SOUTHERN RAILROAD

WHERE TO BOARD:
Leadville Depot, 326 East 7th Street, Leadville.

FOR TICKET INFORMATION:
Leadville, Colorado & Southern R.R. Co., P.O. Box 916, Leadville, CO 80461. Telephone 719-486-3936.

FARES IN 1991:

Adult	Children (4–12)	Children 3 & Under
$16.50	$9.75	Free

Group rates available.

LENGTH OF TRIP:
24 miles round trip, 2½ hours.

DATES OF OPERATION:
Daily mid-June through Labor Day; weekends in September.

SCHEDULE:

Depart	9:30 a.m.	2:00 p.m.
Return	12:15 p.m.	4:45 p.m.

DURANGO & SILVERTON NARROW-GAUGE RAILROAD

WHERE TO BOARD:
Durango Depot at 479 Main Ave. Durango is in southwestern Colorado on US 160.

FOR TICKET INFORMATION:
D&S Railroad, 479 Main Ave., Durango, CO 81301. Telephone: 303-247-2733.

FARES IN 1992:
Silverton Trains round trip: Adults $37.15; Children (5–11) $18.65; Parlor Car (21 yrs. min. age) $63.85.
Cascade Canyon round trip: Adults $31.45; Children $15.70.
Parking lot fees: $5 for cars; $7 for buses $ RVs.

LENGTH OF TRIP:
Silverton—90 miles, 9 hours round trip including 2 hour layover in Silverton. Cascade Canyon—52 miles, 4¹/₄ hours round trip.

DATES OF OPERATION:
May through October.

SCHEDULE:

Durango	LV	RET
to Silverton	7:30 a.m.	4:00 p.m.
	8:30 a.m.	5:25 p.m.
	9:30 a.m.	6:25 p.m.
	10:15 a.m.	6:55 p.m.
Cascade Canyon*	4:40 p.m.	8:59 p.m.

*This train goes to Cascade Canyon, approximately halfway to Silverton, and returns to Durango.

Bus from Silverton to Durango and return by train available June 8 through August 23. Inquire Silverton Depot: 302-387-5416.

SPECIAL EVENTS:
Photographers Special, Sept. 19, 1992.

■ In 1881 the first narrow-gauge steam locomotive clanked, shuddered, and swayed its way into Durango. The very same coal-fired engines and cars, carefully restored, still carry passengers on a forty-five mile adventure through some of the wildest lands in the West. The destination is Silverton, a nineteenth-century mining town with a rough-and-tumble reputation. From Durango, trains chug through the peaceful Animas Valley with its flat green pastures and ranches. There are plenty of horses to be seen and lucky passengers might also see herds of elk wandering through the valley. As the valley narrows, pasture land gives way to forests of shiny scrub oak, aspen, and blue spruce. The train crosses the blue-green Animas River several times, once on an 1880 wrought-iron deck truss bridge. In places the sheer rock walls of the mountains press the tracks onto narrow ledges that drop off hundreds of feet into the river gorge.

Interestingly, the railroads played an important role in the development of skiing in this country. Originally, the long curve-tipped boards we call skis—Norwegian snowshoes—were intended, not for entertainment, but for winter transportation in snowy places such as Switzerland, Scandinavia, or the American Rockies. A pair of Norwegians named Carl Howelsen and Angell Schmidt changed that. They boarded a Denver, Northwestern & Pacific train with their skis shortly before Christmas in 1911 and started a revolution. Stepping off the train at a mountain depot, they found themselves a convenient slope and began to schuss. Following their example, more and more skiers took the trains to reach suitable skiing spots. Resorts grew up at some of the more popular slopes, and after World War II the Denver & Rio Grande Western began to run special ski trains to service them.

Today regular ski trains run from Denver past spectacular rock formations known as "The Flat Irons" and through the Moffat Tunnel to Winter Park. Not just for skiers, the Rio Grande Ski Train serves as a wonderful winter excursion, even for those who have never seen a ski lift and never intend to step onto one. The trains offer a unique and spectacular view of the wintertime Rocky Mountains.

RIO GRANDE SKI TRAIN

WHERE TO BOARD:
Denver Union Station.

FOR TICKET INFORMATION:
Rio Grande Ski Train, 555 17th Street, Suite 2400, Denver, CO 80202. Telephone 303-296-4754.

FARES IN 1991:
Coach $25; first class $40.

LENGTH OF TRIP:
120 miles round trip from Denver to West Portal of Winter Park Resort.

DATES OF OPERATION:
Holiday excursions December 26–28 and February 17. Weekends January 4 to April 5.

SCHEDULE:

LV Denver	7:15 a.m.
AR Winter Park	9:15 a.m.
LV Winter Park	4:15 p.m.
AR Denver	6:15 p.m.

You'll enjoy a unique view of the snowy winter Rockies when you ride the Rio Grande Ski Train. PHOTO BY ROBERT ASHE; COURTESY RIO GRANDE SKI TRAIN.

MANITOU & PIKE'S PEAK RAILWAY

WHERE TO BOARD:

Cog Road Depot, 515 Ruxton Avenue, Manitou Springs. Take exit 141 off I-25 west on US 24 to Manitou Springs. Exit at signs to Cog Railroad and Manitou Springs. Take Manitou Ave. to Ruxton Ave. Turn left, one mile to depot.

FOR TICKET INFORMATION:

Manitou & Pike's Peak Cog Railway, Cog Road Depot, P.O. Box 351, Manitou Springs, CO 80829. Telephone 719-685-5401.

FARES IN 1992:

Round trip fares—Adults $20.50; Children (5–11) $9; Seniors (60+) $18 (pre-Mem. Day wknd & post-Labor Day ONLY). Children under 5 ride free if held on lap. One-way tickets sold on space available basis only. Reservations strongly advised.

LENGTH OF TRIP:

3¼ hours round trip including 40-minute stop at the summit of Pike's Peak.

DATES OF OPERATION:

May through October, weather permitting.

SCHEDULE:

	DEPART	RETURN
Mid-June to mid-Aug.	8:00 a.m.	11:10 a.m.
May thru Oct.	9:20 a.m.	12:30 p.m.
Mid-May thru Sept.	10:40 a.m.	1:50 p.m.
June thru Aug.	Noon	3:10 p.m.
May thru Oct.	1:20 p.m.	4:30 p.m.
June thru Sept.	2:40 p.m.	5:50 p.m.
Mid-June to mid-Aug.	4:00 p.m.	7:10 p.m.
Late June to mid-Aug.	5:20 p.m.	8:30 p.m.

SPECIAL EVENTS:

Baldwin Steam Locomotive #4 will be operated on a very limited basis. Call for info.

For the past one hundred years trains have trundled to the top of Pike's Peak on the world's highest cog railway. Their passengers have enjoyed views usually available only to eagles and bighorn sheep. Mattress manufacturer Zalman G. Simmons—always concerned with comfort—built the railroad after a jostling ride to the top of the mountain by mule. (Some say Simmons wore his customary Prince Albert coat and high silk hat on the trip, which may have added considerably to his discomfort.)

Because the grade was so steep, all construction work on the line had to be done by hand using picks, shovels, and wheelbarrows. In many places the grade was so steep that not even pack animals could be used. Indeed, the train makes one of the steepest climbs in the world. The cog wheels travel on toothed tracks which serve as a sort of ladder enabling the train to climb grades of up to twenty-five percent. When the train hits such a grade, the upper end of the bright red Swiss cog-wheel car stands about twelve feet higher than the lower end. If the thrilling ride won't cause passengers to suck in their breath, then the view from the top of Pike's Peak certainly will: the Garden of the Gods, the majestic Rockies, and a hundred miles of Colorado plains stretching into the purple distance.

Highest cog railway in the world, the Manitou & Pik's Peak takes you to the top.
COURTESY MANITOU & PIKE'S PEAK RAILWAY.

In 1881 the Union Pacific decided to build from Georgetown to the rich but isolated mountain community of Silver Plume. Though only about two miles from Georgetown, Silver Plume stood 638 feet higher in elevation—which meant it might as well have been on the moon. A train running directly from one town to the other would have to climb a grade of over six percent, much too steep for most locomotives. What was worse, the sheer rock walls of Clear Creek (known as Tough Cuss Creek to local miners) left no room for switchbacks. Robert Blickensderfer, an experienced Union Pacific engineer proposed a solution: The tracks would loop back over themselves to gain the necessary elevation within the limited space available.

Once the construction contract was awarded, 200 men immediately set to work on the Loop Line. But the pace of construction dropped off steadily as laborers slipped away into the gold and silver fields where they hoped to strike it rich. The high Devil's Gate bridge took a full month to assemble, the crews hurrying to finish before winter. At the end of November, chief engineer Stanton inspected the bridge. As the Georgetown Courier put it, "The builders finished putting up the immense iron structure last week, but owing to a defect in the riveting, and owing to the fact that the columns of the bridge have been placed wrong, Engineer Stanton will not accept it. . . . "

The truth was the entire bridge had been built backwards: The south supporting tower had been erected on the north side of the bridge and the north tower on the south side. The whole structure had to be torn apart and rebuilt—in the dead of winter—a process that took a full six weeks. Finally, on March 10, 1884, the tracks reached Silver Plume and another silver spike was driven home.

GEORGETOWN LOOP RAILROAD

WHERE TO BOARD:

Devil's Gate Boarding Area—1 mile from downtown Georgetown, west of Denver. Take exit 228 off I-70.

Silver Plume Depot—Take exit 226 off I-70 west of Denver.

FOR TICKET INFORMATION:

Georgetown Loop Railroad, Old Georgetown Station, P.O. Box 217, 1106 Rose Street, Georgetown, CO 80444. Telephone—Old Georgetown Station: 303-670-1686; 303-569-2403. FAX 303-569-2894.

FARES IN 1992:

Railroad Round Trip—Adults $10.50; Children (4–15) $6. Children under 4 free when not occupying a seat.
Mine Tour—Adults $3; Children $1.50
   Mine tours May 25–Sept. 7; board from Silver Plume Depot. Charter & group rates available.

LENGTH OF TRIP:

6¹/₂ miles, 70 minutes.

DATES OF OPERATION:

Weekends beginning May 16. Daily June 13 through August 30. Weekends August 29 through October 4, and early December.

SCHEDULE:

Weekends May 16 & 23, and Aug. 29 through Oct. 4; Holidays; & daily June 13–Aug. 30.
LV Georgetown (round trip)
10:00 & 11:20 a.m., 12:40, 2:00, & 3:20 p.m.
LV Silver Plume (round trip)
9:20 & 10:40 a.m., Noon, 1:20, 2:40, & 4:00 p.m.

Weekdays May 26–June 12 & Aug. 31–Sept. 4
LV Georgetown (round trip)
10:00 & 11:20 a.m., 12:40, & 2:00 p.m.
LV Silver Plume (round trip)
9:20 & 10:40 a.m., Noon, 1:20 & 2:40 p.m.

Weekdays Sept. 8 through Oct. 2
LV Georgetown—12:40 & 2:00 p.m.
LV Silver Plume—Noon, 1:20 & 2:40 p.m.

SPECIAL EVENTS:

Santa's Express (1st two weekends of December). Write for schedule.

NEVADA NORTHERN RAILWAY

WHERE TO BOARD:
East Ely Depot, 1100 Avenue A at 11th Street East. East Ely is in eastern Nevada on US 93.

FOR TICKET INFORMATION:
Nevada Northern Railway Museum, P.O. Box 40, 11th Street at Avenue A, East Ely, NV 89315-0040. Telephone 702-289-2085.

FARES IN 1992:

	Ghost Train Keystone Route	Ghost Train Comb. w/Highliner	Highliner
Adults	$12	$16	$8
Juniors (12–18)	10	14	6
Seniors	10	14	6
Children (5–11)	4	6	3

Twilight Special	One route only	Comb. both routes
Adults	$8	$14
Juniors (12–18)	6	10
Seniors	6	10
Children (5–11)	3	4

Children under 5 ride free when accompanied by an adult.

LENGTH OF TRIP:
Ghost Train of Old Ely—Steam Powered Excursion, 14 miles, 1½ hour round trip. *The Highliner*—Diesel Ore Line Excursion, 22 miles, 1½ hour round trip. *The Twilight Special*—possible combination ticket for both routes.

DATES OF OPERATION:
Specific Saturdays & Sundays May through September. One-hour walking tours are offered May 23–Sept. 6, Wed.–Sun., 9:00 & 11:00 a.m. and 1:30 & 3:30 p.m. $2.50/person (10 & older).

SCHEDULE:

	Saturday	Sunday
Ghost Train	2:30 p.m.	11:00 a.m.
	4:30 p.m.	1:00 p.m.
Highliner	6:30 p.m.	—
Twilight Special	4:30 p.m.*	—
	6:30 p.m.*	—

*One hour earlier beginning August 15.

SPECIAL EVENTS:
"Nevada Northern Raildays," Labor Day Weekend.

■ It was the bonanza at Copper Flats just west of town that put Ely on the map. The metal-heavy rocks beneath the ground here held so much copper that a branch railroad was needed to ship it all out. The line would link Ely and the fabulous copper diggings nearby with the Southern Pacific mainline.

In 1904 engineers began to lay out the route. That winter a series of blizzards brought howling winds and temperatures of −22°F. Young engineers from back east found the cold almost unbearable, especially when their tent stakes, driven in frozen ground, popped out unexpectedly and cold canvas and snow collapsed in the sleepers' faces. The following winter in the Steptoe Valley was even worse. It held up the grading and laying of track, but by July 1906 the line to Ely was completed with a ceremonial copper spike. Ely boomed.

The Nevada Northern then extended tracks to the copper mines. This required blasting a tunnel and building a huge, double-tracked trestle so copper ore from the mines could be carried to the smelters in McGill.

The Nevada Consolidated Copper Company also built an extensive system of pit trains that ran on tracks laid along the terraces of the huge open-pit mines where giant steam shovels scooped out the raw copper ore. The ore was dumped into pit trains and carried over eleven miles of track to the surface, then hauled to McGill where smelters processed 20,000 tons of ore daily.

Today the copper trains are mostly gone, but the Ely "Ghost Train" still offers passengers a close-up look at copper country. The line includes a wonderful collection of original diesel, steam, and electric trains, rolling stock, and original buildings and equipment.

The C&TS, with its sixty-four-mile ride into the heart of the Rockies, offers one of finest scenic railroading experiences in America. The tracks straddle the state line between New Mexico and Colorado. Spiked down in 1880 as the San Juan extension of the Denver & Rio Grande, the narrow-gauge railroad was built to serve rich mining camps in the San Juan hills.

Leaving Antonito Colorado, the C&TS angles southwest over rolling hills and then climbs steadily through aspen groves into the high San Juan range. Passengers are treated to stunning mountain views, the dramatic rock formations at Phantom Curve, and the spectacular Toltec Gorge of the Los Pinas River where the train runs on a shelf blasted from solid rock high above the river. Cresting at 10,015-foot Cumbres Pass, the train drops down a precipitous four percent grade along Wolf Creek where it crosses several bridges into Chama, New Mexico.

The C&TS locomotives and rolling stock are as "old west" as the scenery and its trains have been featured in several western movies. Although some early Colorado Rocky Mountain trains burned wood, coal was the fuel of choice for most steam locomotives. The Baldwin Mikado locomotives at C&TS burn 4,000 pounds of coal and boil 4,000 gallons of water an hour on their trip over the mountains. All that coal is shoveled into the firebox by a single, very sturdy fireman. Coal cars are loaded by means of a tipple at the Chama train yard. Climbing up the pass makes the engines very thirsty, and there are five traditional water towers along the route. These are filled by gravity from springs in the mountains. The echoing whistle, the hiss of steam, and the pungent smell of coal smoke make the Cumbres & Toltec a ride to remember.

CUMBRES & TOLTEC SCENIC RAILROAD

WHERE TO BOARD:
Chama Depot—Chama, New Mexico, on US 84.
Antonito Depot—Antonito, Colorado, on US 285.

FOR TICKET INFORMATION:
Chama Depot, year-round office—Cumbres and Toltec Scenic Railroad, P.O. Box 789, Chama, NM 87520. Telephone 505-756-2151.
Antonito Depot, Memorial Day Weekend through Mid-October—Cumbres and Toltec Scenic Railroad, P.O. Box 668, Antonito, CO 81120. Telephone 719-376-5483.

FARES IN 1992:
Round trip from either Antonito or Chama to the mid-point at Osier—Adults $29; Children (11 & under) $11.
Through trip from either depot with return by van—Adults $45.50; Children (11 and under) $23.
One-way trip from either depot—Adults $39; Children (11 & under) $18.50. Charters available.

LENGTH OF TRIP:
64 miles one way; 6–8 hours depending on options, including layovers and a 60-minute van ride.

DATES OF OPERATION:
Memorial Day Weekend to mid-October.

SCHEDULE:
Two trains operating seven days a week.

FROM ANTONITO DEPOT	DEPART	RETURN
Round trip to Osier	10:00 a.m.	5:00 p.m.
One-way train to Chama return by van*	10:00 a.m.	5:30 p.m.
Van to Chama one-way return by train*	9:15 a.m.	5:00 p.m.
FROM CHAMA DEPOT	DEPART	RETURN
Round trip to Osier	10:30 a.m.	4:30 p.m.
One-way train to Antonito return by van*	10:30 a.m.	6:35 p.m.
Van to Antonito return by train	8:00 a.m.	4:30 p.m.

*One-way passengers may also arrange their own transportation.

EMPIRES

Before they could start work steaming over steel rails and hauling freight in the Far West, locomotives first went to sea. Loaded onto schooners in the East, the iron behemoths were shipped around stormy Cape Horn on a 15,000-mile ocean trek to California. Railroad equipment had no other way to reach California until the final spike was driven at Promontory Point, Utah, in 1869. Options for settlers were also limited. They could choose to take ship like the locomotives, journey through the fever-plagued Isthmus of Panama (long before the Canal), or lug all their worldly possessions to the West in Conestoga wagons. But once the new transcontinental tracks were complete, practically everything reached the West by train. In fact, the railroads could move more goods and people in a single year than all the wagon trains that ever rolled.

Silver Rails, Golden Spike

Almost as soon as the ink was dry on the Louisiana Purchase people began to talk of linking the Atlantic and Pacific by railway. But for decades the idea remained just that—talk. Then in 1849 came the California Gold Rush, and the American urge to go west became a fever. The government sent army surveyors west to pick a route for a transcontinental railroad, but sharpening tensions between the North and South cast a shadow over the process. The country was already on the road to civil war.

One American who gave more thought to building up the country than tearing it apart was Theodore Judah. In 1854 the twenty-eight-year-old railroad construction engineer arrived in California after months of perilous steamboat and land travel across Central America. Judah found this tortuous route only a little faster than his other options—a six-month sail around the tip of South America or a year of rattling westward on a wagon train. The trip left a deep impression on him.

Judah had recently completed the Niagara Gorge Railroad, considered a marvel of engineering, and now he was engaged to build a railroad from Sacramento into the gold-mining country in the rugged Sierra foothills. While designing and building the new line he began to think of bigger things. He envisioned laying a set of tracks that would

Past meets present as a steam locomotive of the White Pass & Yukon line crosses paths with a cruise ship in Skagway, Alaska. COURTESY WHITE PASS & YUKON ROUTE, SKAGWAY, ALASKA.

reach far beyond the Sierras, in fact, right through Donner Pass and onward clear to the Atlantic. In a drugstore he drew up the Articles of Association for the Central Pacific Railroad of California. The CPRC was more imagination than railroad, however. It had no track, no locomotives, and no money. But Judah collared four Sacramento merchants—a grocer, a dry goodsman, and two hardware store clerks and sold them on his dream. In time, he would make the four of them—Leland Stanford, Charles Crocker, Mark Hopkins, and Collis Huntington—rich and powerful beyond their own capacities to dream. Within a decade they would become notorious as the "Big Four," leaders of a railroad "octopus" squeezing money out of the West in general and western farmers and miners in particular. But the money Judah coaxed from his partners was a pittance compared to what he needed for his railway. So he returned to the East and descended on Washington to lobby for federal assistance.

Judah was in luck. The man in the White House was Abraham Lincoln who, in addition to believing in a closely knit Union, was also a business-oriented Republican. Rather than blocking the drive for a transcontinental railroad, the Civil War was putting steam in its boiler. With southern obstructionists removed from Congress, Lincoln rammed through the Pacific Railroad Act, signing the measure on July 1, 1863, the first day of the battle of Gettysburg. The bill divided the transcontinental pie between two companies. The Union Pacific would lay track westward from Omaha and across the Rockies while Judah's own Central Pacific would start from Sacramento and build eastward through the Sierras and across the Great Basin. In return for these efforts, the companies would receive financial aid of up to $48,000 per mile (amounts differed according to the terrain), rights of way, free land, and low-interest loans. Suddenly, with the stroke of a pen, Judah had his railroad. Wiring his partners in Sacramento, the still youthful engineer crowed, "We have drawn the elephant. Now let us see if we can harness him up."

What the new railroad tycoons would harness was not so much an elephant as one of the world's oldest motives—greed. From beginning to end, graft and scandal would haunt the building of the transcontinental railway. Federal construction money for the Union Pacific was drawn from a special bank or "super fund" known as the Crédit Mobilier. Corrupt congressmen, federal officials, and railroad trustees used the Mobilier as a financial feeding trough. The directors of the Mobilier were those most likely to benefit from spending its monies. "The members of it are in Congress . . . trustees . . . directors . . . stockholders . . . contractors," said one astonished journalist. "In Washington they wrote the subsidies, in New York they receive them, upon the plains they expend them . . . they receive money into one hand and pay it into another. . . ."

Judah returned from Washington to find the Big Four already building the railroad and wringing it for every possible dime. The Four had launched their own construction company. Then, in their role as railroad trustees, awarded themselves the lucrative transcontinental contract. Using a report written by a compliant geologist named Josiah Whitney, they had managed to convince Lincoln and his advisors that the Sierras began, not in the foothills, but many miles further west. That way they received the highest government subsidies even though they were laying track over nearly level ground. The Four boasted that their "pertinacity and Lincoln's faith moved mountains."

The highest of the Sierra's real and immovable mountains was eventually named for Whitney, but Judah's reward for having fathered the nation's transcontinental railway would be far less noble. Judah was horrified by his partners' greed and lack of scruples. When he protested, they forced him out of the company, buying up his stock for $100,000. Judah decided to return to Washington in search of the money and political support he needed to regain control. He never got there. Ironically, he was once more forced to travel through Central America, and in Panama he caught yellow fever and died.

The federal grants and assistance to the two railroads included thousands of acres of land which once belonged, if that is the appropriate word, to the Indians. Located primarily in mountain country or desert, much of the land was marginal, but it rapidly increased in value once the railroad was built. Not surprisingly, the Indians received little or no compensation beyond a few small gifts or an occasional free ride behind

Up close and personal with Union Pacific's No. 8444. DUNCAN RICHARDS.

California offers several outstanding scenic railroading options, including the "Super Skunk" train shown here. Its unusual gas-powered steam engine reportedly could be smelled before it could be seen—hence the nickname.
PHOTO BY BOB VON NORMANN; COURTESY CALIFORNIA WESTERN RAILROAD, FORT BRAGG, CALIFORNIA.

A beautiful diesel in beautiful country. COURTESY MOUNT HOOD RAILROAD, HOOD RIVER, OREGON.

the iron horse. Perhaps the plains Indians should have followed the lead of their Iroquois cousins in the east. The Iroquois demanded a chunk of hard cash from the Erie Railroad before allowing its tracks to cross their land. Railroad bargainers tried to cut the price by pointing out the rockiness of the land. Since it was no good for growing corn or potatoes, they felt it should be of little worth to the Iroquois. The tribe's wily chief thought about this for a moment and then replied, "It pretty good for railroad." The Erie paid.

Out West, the Union Pacific was much less generous. Railroad tycoon Collis Huntington cut a remarkable deal with the Paiutes and Shoshones. "We gave the old chiefs a pass each, good on the passenger cars," said Huntington. "And we told our men to let the common Indians ride on the freight cars whenever they saw fit." The more warlike Sioux didn't ask for or receive passes. It was clear enough to them that they and their brothers were being bilked. They picked off advance parties and burned a few trains, tossing the tomahawked bodies of the crews into the flames. The government rushed in cavalry units but escorts were small.

As General George Crook remarked, it was difficult to surround three Indians with one cavalry trooper. So Union Pacific Railroad laborers, many of whom still wore their blue or gray uniforms from the recently concluded war, carried carbines, rifles, and revolvers.

Much of the Union Pacific was built by Grenville Dodge, a Civil War general. After the war, Dodge spent two years locating the railroad right of way and clearing out hostile Indians from the Black Hills and Wasatch Mountains. He took complete control of the Union Pacific construction effort in May of 1866, and by the time fall snows halted construction, his crews had spiked down 293 miles of track.

Railroad backers bothered Dodge more than Indians. Perhaps because Dodge's 10,000-man workforce was much larger and better equipped than the U.S. Cavalry, the Sioux mostly kept their distance. Hundreds of miles out front of the actual construction crews were the surveyors and engineers who chose the route. Next came a location crew to pinpoint an exact site for the tracks. Graders followed and after them the laborers who actually laid down the rails. Bridge-building crews worked at least twenty-five miles ahead of track layers, throwing up spidery spans across the Green River, the North Platte, Lodgepole Creek, the Bear River, and hundreds of other rivers and streams. The operation was very military in its precision.

Bringing in the mountains of supplies needed to keep the work

FIRST EXCURSION TRAIN IN ALASKA
SKAGWAY, JULY 21, 1898

Railroading in Alaska was truly an adventure. The first train to operate there was this one, on July 21, 1898; it ran a passenger excursion from Skagway out four miles (to the end of the track) and returned. COURTESY WHITE PASS & YUKON ROUTE, SKAGWAY, ALASKA.

moving forward was a logistical challenge not unlike that faced by the commander of an army on the march. But Dodge was up to it. A steady stream of wagons hauled in provisions while drovers minded herds of stringy longhorns to keep plenty of beef on workers' metal plates. Construction material had to be shipped from back east over a single line of track from Omaha.

Telegraph communication kept Dodge informed of progress and allowed work crews to order supplies as needed. Telegraph lines followed the tracks wherever they went, but their poles sometimes came down almost as fast as they were put up. Itchy Buffalo often knocked down poles while using them as scratching posts. Indians coveted telegraph wire for use in making bracelets. As a result, telegraph service on the line was chancy, and orders for provisions and construction material might take weeks to fill. To cut down on supply problems, Dodge's construction bosses put together a traveling train city of twenty or more cars that carried everything—carpentry, harness-making, and machine shops, kitchens, bunkhouses, offices, a telegraph car and tank cars for water.

The tracks went down in assembly-line style. Supply trains traveled as far west as possible along the newly laid single track and dumped their loads of rails, ties, spikes, switches, and supplies. Small horse-drawn flatcars sometimes driven by children carried the material to the last completed section of rail. Out ahead the ties would go down, five each to a twenty-eight-foot rail. Then the "iron men" would heft the 500- to 700-pound rails and drop them in place, lined up to proper gauge. The horse-drawn flatcar would already be inching along on this newest rail with more supplies while men with sledges pounded in the spikes, three strokes to the spike, ten spikes to the rail, 400 rails to a mile. By the late spring of 1866, workers had become so efficient they could lay a mile of track a day. In time, Dodge's crews could put down two or even three miles of track a day. But a Central Pacific crew set the mileage record: To win a wager, they once laid ten miles of track in a single day.

Who were these railroad workers? Some were soldiers still wearing their blue or gray uniforms; some were Irish, German, or Polish immigrants barely (if at all) able to speak English; some were former slaves, some Indians, some ex-convicts. And following them was a movable city of gamblers, saloon keepers, and prostitutes. The workers called it "Hell on Wheels." General Dodge did little to interfere with the party train until it got so violent that some of his men were killed. Then he cleaned it up vigilante style.

Meanwhile, the Central Pacific had labor problems of a different sort. Charles Crocker, one of the Big Four, took over as construction boss. Accompanied by a Chinese valet wherever he went, Crocker constantly berated his workers, who tended to drift back to the California gold fields as soon as they had a few railroad dollars in their pockets. Finally Crocker hit on the idea of hiring Chinese laborers. They were small in stature, averaging only about 110 pounds, but hadn't they built the Great Wall of China? So Crocker argued with his partners. And unlike European immigrants, particularly the hard-drinking and hard-fighting Irish, Chinese laborers were gentle and kept out of trouble. They set up a neat camp, cooked their own rice, and worked a twelve-hour day. Crocker's Oriental laborers worked so hard that he rounded up all the Chinese he could find in San Francisco and even advertised in Canton so that he could import more workers from China.

In America, these Chinese workers accomplished feats almost as impressive as those of their ancestors who built the Great Wall. Chipping away at solid granite, they tunneled through the Sierras and under Donner Pass. Dangling over cliffs in wicker baskets, they drilled holes for the highly unstable and dangerous explosive nitroglycerine. Much of the work was done at altitudes of a mile or more in driving rains and blizzards. To bring supplies to work sites as many as five locomotives were sometimes needed to push a snowplow through drifts of up to thirty feet. Many workers froze to death or were crushed in avalanches. At least four times great mountain snow ledges collapsed onto the work camp carrying men, animals, buildings, and supplies into canyons where they were buried until spring.

For all their accomplishments, the Chinese were often treated little better than animals. In June of 1867, 2,000 Chinese workers went on strike demanding shorter work days and pay equal to that of white laborers. Crocker ruthlessly broke the strike, and although the Chinese laid the last rail of the transcontinental railroad, they were scarcely mentioned in the speeches at Promontory Point.

By June of 1868, the Central Pacific tracks had broken through the Sierras and now stretched from Sacramento to Nevada. Meanwhile, near Sherman, Wyoming, the Union Pacific tracks had crested the Rockies. Now both railroads pushed on rapidly across the relatively level Great Basin. Since the railroads received fat federal subsidies for every mile of track laid, the two companies ignored their original agreement to link their lines. They kept building right past each other, constructing parallel tracks through Utah and Nevada. Soon the rival work gangs were dynamiting each other's grades and harrying each other with pot shots or tumbling boulders. The UP and CP were slugging it out in the more genteel arena of Washington, D.C., as well. There, political pressure finally put a stop to the fighting. Promontory Point, Utah, six miles west of Odgen, was selected as the official meeting place for the transcontinental lines.

Promontory Point was a shanty town, hardly a dignified place to drive the last spike into an historic rail line linking east to west. But that is where the UP and CP agreed to meet for the spike-driving ceremony on May 10, 1869. The two railroads were still at odds, but officials of both companies were determined to put on a good face for the event. The whisky and oratory flowed freely as a representative from each railroad

The challenges of railroad-building in Alaska are summarized in this 1899 photo: tunnels, trestles, and snow. Glacier Gorge lies below.
COURTESY WHITE PASS & YUKON ROUTE.

TUNNEL ON THE WHITE PASS AND YUKON ROUTE

stood poised with a hammer. Each hammer blow was to be transmitted across the country by telegraph. As well-known photographer A.J. Russell prepared to capture the scene for posterity, his helper yelled "Shoot!" The Chinese misunderstood the helper's meaning and dove for cover. As a result Russell's famous golden spike photograph is nearly devoid of Chinese faces.

From coast to coast Americans waited by the telegraph to signal the hammer blows and set church bells ringing and bands playing in towns across the country. Western Union primed its telegraph operators nationwide for one of history's first managed media events:

> TO EVERYBODY: KEEP QUIET. WHEN THE
> LAST SPIKE IS DRIVEN WE WILL SAY "DONE."
> DON'T BREAK THE CIRCUIT, BUT WATCH
> FOR THE BLOWS OF THE HAMMER.
>
> Promontory Telegraph:
>
> ALMOST READY. HATS OFF. PRAYER IS
> BEING OFFERED.
>
> Chicago Telegraph;
>
> WE UNDERSTAND. ALL ARE READY IN THE
> EAST.
>
> Promontory Telegraph:
>
> ALL READY NOW. THE SPIKE WILL SOON BE
> DRIVEN. THE SIGNAL WILL BE THREE DOTS
> FOR THE COMMENCEMENT OF THE BLOWS.

Leland Stanford, biggest of the Big Four, strode forward, a solid silver hammer in his hand. A hush fell over the assembled dignitaries, politicians, mountain men, prostitutes, Irish and Chinese laborers. No sound could be heard but the hissing of the two engines facing each other on the track, one CP and the other UP.

Stanford swung—and missed.

People laughed, but the excited telegraph operator sent his signal anyway and set bands playing in towns more than a thousand miles away. The locomotives inched forward until they touched and their

Incredible Cheakamus Canyon. COURTESY BC RAIL, VANCOUVER, BRITISH COLUMBIA.

engineers stepped down to break bottles of champagne on each other's engines. After millions of hammer blows had rung out across the prairies and through the mountains, the 1,780-mile construction project was over. Ironically, it ended not with the ring of metal striking metal, but with the shattering of glass.

The railroads, their tycoons, and the engineers became national heroes, but they did not remain so for long. Congress already had the financial practices of the infamous Crédit Mobilier under investigation. Soon the American people realized they had been robbed blind. Summing up public opinion, Senator George Hoar noted sadly that the "national triumph" of the transcontinental, "the greatest railroad in the world . . . uniting two great seas," had been turned to shame by Congressional reports proving that "every step of that mighty enterprise had been taken in fraud."

Even so, people could now travel coast to coast in a railroad car if they had the time the money—and were hardy souls.

O n May 23, 1870, a train stood waiting at the Boston & Albany station, its locomotive steamed up and ready to roll. More than 50,000 people had crowded into the station for a glimpse of this elegant train which was about to make history—the nation's first transcontinental railway run. Like Lindbergh's flight across the Atlantic more than a generation afterwards, this journey "from Faneuil Hall to the Golden Gate" fired the imagination of Americans.

A gentlemanly list of passengers—writers, lawyers, and members of the Boston Board of Trade—were taking their wives and children on a trip from the extra-civilized environs of Boston all the way to the Wild West and back again. They would travel in eight of what George Pullman called "the most elegant cars ever pulled over an American railway . . . equipped with every desirable accessory that may tend in the least to promote the ease of the passengers." The baggage car held five ice closets and a refrigerator to provide chefs with ingredients for the sumptuous, multi-course meals served on board. Two hotel cars (appropriately dubbed the Revere and the Arlington) provided passengers with the comforts of home while a smoking car, sleeping car, drawing room car, dining car, and commissary car filled out the train.

The train even had its own newspaper to cover the journey—the *Transcontinental* published on a Gordon printing press kept in the baggage car. From a paneled office in the smoking car, editor E.R. Steele chronicled the glories of the trip beneath a masthead featuring a train

From Sea to Sea

The Napa Valley Wine Train is your ticket to dining elegance as you roll through California's famous wine country. COURTESY NAPA VALLEY WINE TRAIN.

Century-old locomotives still have to stop to take on water for their boilers. PHOTO BY BOB VON NORMANN; COURTESY CALIFORNIA WESTERN RAILROAD.

with eight cars prominently labeled "Pullman Palace Car Company." The masthead showed the train rolling across plains under the watchful eyes of an Indian with feathers, a blanket, and a scowling, cigar-store countenance. Steele's writing was no less stylized than the masthead; it fairly sparkled with the romance of his railroad adventure in the West.

When the Boston train pulled out of the station to the cheers of an enthusiastic multitude, editor Steele compared the "All aboard to San Francisco" of the train conductor to the "yes" of Helen of Troy. On board Mr. Steele had plenty of highbrow folks to appreciate his flowery prose. In addition to a fine assortment of immaculately dressed Brahmins, there was an impressive array of dignitaries. Among them was George Pullman, whose shrewd publicity of this trip on Pullman Palace cars helped make his name, his company, and his passenger cars a railroad standard almost as widely accepted as the standard-gauge spacing of rails.

Gentlemen on the train could stop in the mirrored and paneled barber shop for a trim and a shave, play a rubber of whist or euchre at the card tables in the smoking car, or buy drinks for one another at the wine room bar. Ladies could take tea in the gilt and velvet drawing room, select a book of poetry, fiction, or history from the ladies' library (there was a separate gentlemen's library), or perhaps play selections from Stephen Foster's songbook on one of the "improved Burdett organs."

Traveling steadily westward, the passengers saw a great land in transition, a western America just beginning to fully open to settlement. Rolling over a steam-powered drawbridge they marveled at an experience still awe-inspiring for travelers today—crossing the Mississippi. Beyond the "big ditch," the New Englanders watched in wonder as a seeming ocean of rich farmland passed outside their windows. They saw Cheyenne, Wyoming, where three years before there had been only one house, and Sherman, a rugged mountain town built at an altitude of 8,235 feet and named for the U.S. Army's tallest general. They crossed the Great Divide and the Great American Desert. Ladies sipped lemonade and thrilled at the sight of buffalo, pronghorn antelope, and blue-uniformed cavalry detachments.

At Ogden, Utah, a Mormon town, the passengers were astonished by what these religious folk had accomplished—raising flowers, barns, and buildings in the desert. Brigham Young himself boarded the train along with various Mormon bishops and apostles to share a meal in the gilded splendor of the dining car. At supper, he told the Boston party he was sixty-nine years old, had sixteen wives and forty-nine children, and had attended school only eleven days in his whole life.

The elegant train rolled on through the passes. At last they steamed over Summit Pass and on down to San Francisco. There they emptied a bottle of Massachusetts Bay water into the Pacific—with all due ceremony, of course.

The easterners loved California. They saw giant sequoias, goldmines, and sunsets over the ocean. But at length, when the time came to board the train and head for Boston, most were glad. There was still much to see on the way home. In Bitter Creek they saw an ox drover with an eighteen-foot blacksnake whip. In Cheyenne, Buckskin Joe regaled them with stories of his prowess as an Indian fighter, hunter, trader, and trapper. Out on the prairies, a swarm of grasshoppers covered the tracks to such a depth they almost stopped the train. The rail journey between two separate worlds ended in Boston six weeks to the day after it had begun. The conclusion of the adventure left some at a loss for words, but not editor Steele. He finished off the final issue of his *Transcontinental* with a cheer: "Hurrah for the railroad!"

Somewhat better equipped than his predecessors, an on-board chef today can dish up gourmet fare. COURTESY NAPA VALLEY WINE TRAIN, NAPA, CALIFORNIA.

In 1896 Skookum Jim Mason lifted a pan from Bonanza Creek and found it awash in tiny golden flakes. Thus began the great Klondike gold rush. Thousands of would-be millionaires trekked to the Dawson gold fields through Dead Horse Pass on a trail so narrow that two pack horses could not pass side by side. Three thousand hapless pack animals sacrificed their lives on the steep, treacherous trail and gave the pass its name. Obviously a railroad was needed.

The distance from Skagway to White Horse in the Yukon was only 110 track miles, but laying in the new line was one of the most difficult railroad construction projects ever undertaken. Rails, rolling stock, tools, supplies, and experienced laborers all were practically nonexistent in this remote corner of the continent. Everything had to be brought in by sea from the "states." Construction crews—mostly would-be prospectors paid as little as 30¢ a day—fought the mountains and the elements every day. Deep snows and sub-zero temperatures held them back in winter while floods, mudslides, and clouds of mosquitoes hampered them in summer. There were glaciers and chasms to span, tunnels to bore, and steep mountain grades to mount. In spite of all the obstacles, they had hacked out the line as far as Lake Benett by 1899. From there steamers could take passengers and freight to the gold fields.

Eventually, the railway ran all the way to the Yukon, and countless thousands of ever-hopeful prospectors rocked along in its coaches. Today passengers can follow the same railway trail into gold country. The WP&Y operates both round trip excursions and through passenger service to the Yukon. Trains roll out of Skagway behind old No. 73, a Baldwin 2-8-2, but in the mountains diesels take over to tackle the steep grades.

White Pass & Yukon Route

WHERE TO BOARD:
Railroad Depot, 2nd and Spring streets, Skagway, Alaska.

FOR TICKET INFORMATION:
WP&Y Route, Box 435, Skagway, AK 99840. Telephone: 800-343-7373, or 907-983-2217.

FARES IN 1992:
Round trip to White Pass Summit: Adult $72; Children (12 & under) $36.
Through service: Adult $92; Children $46.

LENGTH OF TRIP:
Summit Excursion—41 miles, 3 hours round trip.

DATES OF OPERATION:
Daily mid-May to late September, conditions permitting.

SCHEDULE:

Summit Excursion	LV	RET
	8:45 a.m.	11:45 a.m.
	1:15 p.m.	4:15 p.m.

Group and charter excursions available.

Still on the frontier, Skagway, Alaska, looks pretty much as it did at the turn of the century. COURTESY WHITE PASS & YUKON ROUTE.

BC RAIL LIMITED

WHERE TO BOARD:
1311 West First Street, North Vancouver.

FOR TICKET INFORMATION:
BC Rail, P.O. Box 8770, Vancouver, BC V6B 4X6. Telephone:
604-631-3500.

FARES IN 1991:
Round trip to Squamish: Adult $28.50; Seniors & Youth $24; Children
$15. Children under age five ride free.
Charters & excursions available.

LENGTH OF TRIP:
80 miles, 6 hours round trip.

DATES OF OPERATION:
Late May through September.

SCHEDULE:

LV N. Vancouver 10:00 a.m.	ARR Squamish 11:50 a.m.
LV Squamish 2:00 p.m.	ARR N. Vancouver 4:00 p.m.

Boarding begins at 9:00 a.m.; seating is first-come, first-served.

■ Beginning in 1912, the Pacific Great Eastern Railroad Company pushed tracks eastward from Vancouver into the heart of British Columbia. As with many western railroads, its construction was a tribute to human ingenuity and endurance. Mountains, rivers, and snow fields blocked the way. Supply shortages, labor disputes, and empty company treasuries impeded progress. But the PGE gradually extended its tracks 463 miles north to Prince George in central British Columbia. By 1914 trains were rolling, providing remote northern camps and villages with access to civilization. The PGE trains "from nowhere to nowhere" served as a lifeline for settlers, trappers, ranchers, miners, and lumberjacks. Today BC Rail is still a vital link for denizens of the backcountry, and it offers passengers a unique way to enjoy some of the splendors of this road-shy province.

Anderson Lake and the Canadian Rockies provide scenic accompaniment for
a ride on BC Rail. COURTESY BC RAIL, VANCOUVER, BRITISH COLUMBIA.

Named for its original self-powered gas engines—"You could smell 'em before you could see 'em"—the Skunk train began service in 1885 as a logging railroad. Still an operating passenger service with stops to deliver groceries and mail along the way, the Skunk also runs historic steam and diesel logging locomotives from Fort Bragg on the coast to Willits. These trains cross over thirty bridges and trestles and pass through two long mountain tunnels as well as several tunnel-like redwood groves.

CALIFORNIA WESTERN RAILROAD

WHERE TO BOARD:
Skunk Depot, Main & Pine streets in Fort Bragg.

FOR TICKET INFORMATION:
California Western Railroad, P.O. Box 907, Fort Bragg, CA 95437. Telephone: Recorded information 415-399-1194; Information & reservations 707-964-6371.

FARES IN 1991:
Full Day: Adult $23; Children $11.
Half Day & One Way: Adult $18.50; Children $9.
Children under five may ride free unless occupying a revenue seat.

LENGTH OF TRIP:
40 miles one way; full day round trip 6–7 hours; half day round trip 3 hours.

DATES OF OPERATION:
Year-round.

SCHEDULE:
OFF SEASON (Jan. through mid-June & mid-Sept. through Dec.)
Full Day Round trips
   Daily from Fort Bragg depart 9:20 a.m.; return 4:00 p.m.
Half-Day Round trips
   Leave Fort Bragg 10 a.m. & 2:00 p.m.
      Available Sat. & Sun. in Jan., Feb., March, & Dec. Daily
      April to mid-June & mid-Sept. to Nov. 30, and most holiday
      weekends.

SUMMER SEASON (mid-June through mid-September)
Depart Fort Bragg; available daily
   9:20 a.m.—Full, Half and One Way
   1:35 p.m.—Half & One Way

Depart Willits; available daily
   8:50 a.m.—Full, Half and One Way
   1:45 p.m.—Half and One Way

ROARING CAMP & BIG TREES NARROW-GAUGE RAILROAD

WHERE TO BOARD:
Roaring Camp on Graham Hill Road in Felton, 6 miles inland from Santa Cruz, or Santa Cruz Beach Boardwalk.

FOR TICKET INFORMATION:
Santa Cruz, Big Trees, & Pacific Railway Co., P.O. Box G-1, Felton, CA 95018. Telephone 408-335-4484.

FARES IN 1992:
Adults $12.95; Children (3–15) $8.95.
Group rates available.

LENGTH OF TRIP:
15 mile, 2½ hours round trip to beach at Santa Cruz.

DATES OF OPERATION:
Weekends and holidays May 23–June 12; Daily June 13–Sept. 7.
Weekends and holidays Sept. 8–Nov. 1.

SCHEDULE:
Train leaves from Felton at 10:30 a.m. & 2:50 p.m.
Departs Santa Cruz at noon.

■ This excursion train is part of the Santa Cruz, Big Trees & Pacific Railway Company which operates as a common carrier from Santa Cruz to Felton and Olympia. Redwoods—some 250 feet tall and ten to fifteen feet in diameter—and the romantic history of the gold fields are the main attractions. In 1842 Isaac Graham, a nephew of Daniel Boone, discovered a single gold nugget worth $32,000 at the nearby settlement of Roaring Camp. However, it was not gold but lumber that brought railroading to the area. In 1869 the first narrow-gauge tracks were laid to Felton to bring lumber down from the hills to the wharves at Santa Cruz.

Today passengers travel through giant redwood, pine, tanbark oak, and madrone forests drenched by eighty inches of rain a year. Once into the San Lorenzo River Gorge, the line courses down the west side of a stunning granite and sandstone whitewater canyon, over wooden trestles, steel bridges, and deep gorges.

Big trees are indeed the attraction for passengers on the Santa Cruz, Big Trees & Pacific Railway. Nearby, the Roaring Camp & Big Trees Narrow Gauge offers a taste of gold-mining history. COURTESY SANTA CRUZ, BIG TREES & PACIFIC RAILWAY.

The Napa Valley Wine Train whisks passengers back in time to an era when railroads offered luxury travel and dining cars were as opulent as any uptown restaurant. Brunch, luncheon, and dinner are served in white-linen style aboard the elegantly refurbished 1917 Pullman coaches. Afterward, diners savor coffee, dessert, and cordials in a lounge car bedecked in hand-rubbed mahogany, etched glass, and polished brass trim. The cars, painted burgundy, champagne, and grape-leaf green, reflect the scenery as the train makes its thirty-six-mile run past twenty-six wineries.

NAPA VALLEY WINE TRAIN

WHERE TO BOARD:
NVWT main depot at 1275 McKinstry Street in Napa.

From San Francisco: Head north across the Golden Gate Bridge, take Highway 101 to Highway 37. Follow Highway 37 to Highway 121 then head north on 121 into Napa. At the Highway 29/121 split, take the right fork, Highway 121, toward Lake Berryessa. Follow Highway 121 until it splits at Soscol Ave. Take the left fork, Soscol Ave., then turn right on First St. Turn left on McKinstry St. Depot is on the left.

From the East Bay: Take Highway 80 East toward Sacramento. After you cross the Carquinez Bridge, get on Highway 29 north to Napa. When Highway 29 splits with Highway 121, the Silverado Trail, take the right fork toward Lake Berryessa. Follow Highway 121 until it splits at Soscol Ave. Take the left fork, Soscol Ave., then turn right on First St. Turn left on McKinstry St. Depot is on the left.

FOR TICKET INFORMATION:
NVWT, 1275 McKinstry St., Napa, CA 94559. Telephone: 800-427-4124, or 707-253-2111. Group & charters 707-253-0920.

FARES IN 1992:
Round trip train fare $29 per person.
Meals: Brunch & lunch $22–25 per person;
          Four-course deluxe dinner $45 per person.
Train fare reduced to $14.50/person with dinner.
Fri., Sat,. & Sun. lunch trains have a deli car where an a la carte menu is available. Train fare is $20 per person.
All taxes and gratuities included.

LENGTH OF TRIP:
36 miles, 3 hours round trip.

DATES OF OPERATION:
Year-round.

SCHEDULE:

Luncheon Train	LV	RET
Sat. & Sun.	12:30 p.m.	3:30 p.m.
Mon.–Fri.	11:30 a.m.	2:30 p.m.
Dinner Train		
Tue.–Sat.	6:30 p.m.	10:00 p.m.
Sunday	6:00 p.m.	9:30 p.m.
Brunch Train		
Sat. & Sun.	9:00 a.m.	11:30 a.m.

CALIFORNIA STATE RAILROAD MUSEUM

WHERE TO "BOARD":
Second and "I" streets, Old Sacramento.

FOR INFORMATION:
CSRM, 111 "I" Street, Sacramento, CA 98514.
Telephone: 916-448-4466.

ADMISSION IN 1991:
Adult $5; children (6–12) $2; under age 6 free.

DATES OF OPERATION:
Year-round.

SCHEDULE:
Daily 10:00 a.m.–5:00 p.m. except Thanksgiving, Christmas, & New
Year's Day.

SPECIAL EVENTS:
Living History Programs, Steam-powered excursion trains (May through
Sept.), Special exhibits year-round, U.S. National Hand Car Races.

■ It was in Sacramento at Huntington & Hopkins Hardware that Theodore Judah persuaded four little-known Californians to invest in his wild railroad construction scheme. They would later be known as the "Big Four," as Judah's dream became the Central Pacific Railroad. Mile Post One of the transcontinental line stands right here at the California State Railroad Museum. One of the finest railroad museums in the country, the CSRM displays over thirty locomotives and cars. The hardware store is included among its exhibits. The Sacramento Southern Railroad runs a six-mile excursion along the Sacramento River powered by an unusual 1920 Lima 0-6-0.

An 1873 Virginia & Truckee locomotive is part of the restored rolling stock at the California State Railroad Museum. COURTESY CALIFORNIA STATE RAILROAD MUSEUM.

■ Presently the only operating railroad in the Hawaiian Islands, the LK&P chugs through sugar cane fields. A narrow-gauge, steam-powered replica of an 1890s sugar cane train, it carries passengers past 5,799-foot Mt. Puu Kukii. The views include distant neighboring islands and the Pioneer sugar mill at the old whaling port of Lahaina.

Hawaii's "sugar cane train" chugs along on an elevated trestle through the cane fields. COURTESY LAHAINA, KAANAPALI & PACIFIC RAILROAD.

LAHAINA · MAUI · HAWAII

LAHAINA-KAANAPALI & PACIFIC RAILROAD

WHERE TO BOARD:
Lahaina Station (Lahaina); Puukolii Road Station (West Maui Resort Area); Kaanapali Station (trolley bus from Kaanapali hotels).

FOR TICKET INFORMATION:
LK&P Railroad, P.O. Box 816, Lahaina, HI 96767-0816.
Telephone: 808-661-0089.

FARES IN 1992:
Round trip: Adult $11; Children (3–12) $5.50.
One way: Adult $7.50; Children (3–12) $3.75.
Babes in arms ride free.

LENGTH OF TRIP:
12 miles, 1 hour trip.

DATES OF OPERATION:
Year-round except Thanksgiving & Christmas.

SCHEDULE:

Departures	Puukolii	Kaanapali	Lahaina
	8:55 a.m.	9:10 a.m.	9:45 a.m.
	10:15 a.m.	10:30 a.m.	11:05 a.m.
	11:35 a.m.	11:45 a.m.	12:40 p.m.
	1:10 p.m.	1:25 p.m.	2:00 p.m.
	2:30 p.m.	2:45 p.m.	3:20 p.m.
	3:50 p.m.	4:05 p.m.	4:40 p.m.*

*Last train, one way only, Lahaina to Puukolii.

MOUNT HOOD RAILROAD

WHERE TO BOARD:
MHRR Depot, in Hood River, exit 63 off I-84, 63 miles east of Portland.

FOR TICKET INFORMATION:
Mount Hood Railroad, 110 Railroad Ave., Hood River, OR 97031. Telephone: 503-386-3556.

FARES IN 1992:
Hood River to Parkdale: Adult $17; Seniors (60+) $15; Children (2–11) $10.

Hood River to Odell: Adult $10; Seniors (60+) $8; Children (2–11) $6.

LENGTH OF TRIP:
Hood River to Parkdale—44 miles, 4 hours round trip; Hood River to Odell—17 miles, 2 hours round trip.

DATES OF OPERATION:
April through October.

SCHEDULE:

	To Parkdale		To Odell	
	LV	RET	LV	RET
	10:00 a.m.	2:00 p.m.	3:00 p.m.	5:00 p.m.
April–May 24	Tue.-Sun		Sat. & Sun	
May 25–Sept. 13	Daily		Daily	
Sept. 14–Nov. 1	Tue.-Sun.		Sat. & Sun.	
Winter—By special charter.				

SPECIAL EVENTS:
Easter Egg Train, May Day Festival, Father's Day Surprise, Western Train Robbery, Harvest Festival.

■ Handsome red, yellow, and blue diesels leave the 1911 depot to follow the Hood River, climb through forests, and cross upland valley orchards. The Fruit Blossom special pushes rather than pulls the passenger and freight cars up the three percent grade and around the switchbacks. The destination is the Hood River Valley where orchards stretch from horizon to horizon and Mt. Hood and Mt. Adams stand snow-capped in the distance.

A working freight and passenger line with more than 400 miles of track through logging and farming country, the Washington Central Railroad also operates the "Spirit of Washington" dinner train. Passengers can enjoy an elegant dinner in antique dining cars while the train rolls over bridges and through rugged Yakima Canyon.

Appetizing scenery is just one of the appeals for passengers on the "Spirit of Washington" dinner train.
COURTESY WASHINGTON CENTRAL RAILROAD.

RENTON · WASHINGTON

"SPIRIT OF WASHINGTON" DINNER TRAIN

WHERE TO BOARD:
Renton Depot, South 4th Street and Burnett Avenue.

FOR TICKET INFORMATION:
Spirit of Washington Dinner Train, South 4th Street and Burnett Avenue, Renton, WA 98057. Telephone: 1-800-876-7245 (RAIL).

FARES IN 1991:
Dinner: $55 per person
Lunch/Brunch: $45 per person
Dome Car: $10 extra

LENGTH OF TRIP:
3½ hour round trip.

DATES OF OPERATION:
Year-round.

SCHEDULE:
Tuesday through Friday dinner train leaves 6:30 p.m.
Saturday lunch train leaves 12:00 noon.
Saturday dinner train leaves 6:00 p.m.
Sunday brunch train leaves 11:00 a.m.
Sunday dinner train leaves 5:00 p.m.